Thank You for purchasing *Business Development is Everyone's Business*! We appreciate your order and hope you'll benefit from the ideas in the book.

If you know of others who might be interested in buying a copy of *Business Development is Everyone's Business*, we make it easy for you. Just go to PDC's web site at www.performancedevelopment.net to the "What's New" section. You will find an order form that can be printed off and returned by fax at

(317) 335-3291. Phone orders are also appreciated.

For your information, we are available for speaking and consulting projects. We can do 20-minute presentations, one-hour keynotes, and up to 6-hour workshops. The topic is very well received with a lively presentation of the six principles and examples. If you or someone you know is interested in booking a speaker or trainer on *Business Development is Everyone's Business*, give us a call at (317) 335-2100.

Thanks again for your confidence and support!

Linda Sparks & Kris Butler

Co-Authors, *Business Development is Everyone's Business*

Linda Spark

Kris Butler

What Others Are Saying About This Book

"I have had a difficult time finding business books on the topic of customer service that aren't retail in nature. *Business Development is Everyone's Business* is definitely written for <u>all</u> businesses."
--Steve Gore, Senior Business Analyst, Indiana Mills and Manufacturing, Inc.

"There isn't anyone in an organization who shouldn't be concentrating on creating more sales. *Business Development is Everyone's Business* is a book that will tell you how to get employees on board."
--Jack Sweeney, President, Langsenkamp Manufacturing

"Being old school, I was hesitant to buy in to the *Business Development is Everyone's Business* philosophy. After reading the book, I am very excited about the opportunity to try this within my company."
--Ronald Albright, President, BrightVisions, Inc.

"This book is "must" reading! Anyone not following these ideas and strategies is trying to run their business with their eyes closed."
--Jerry Wilson, CSP, Author, *Word-of-Mouth Marketing*

Business Development is

Everyone's

Business

Linda Sparks and Kris Butler

Business Development is Everyone's Business
by Linda Sparks and Kris Butler

"Business Development is EVERYONE'S Business™" is a trademark of Performance Development Company (PDC) and is just one of a family of custom products including workshops, keynote presentations, organizational assessments, and self-administered learning kits.

Published by:
Performance Development Company
9801 Fall Creek Rd., PMB 347
Indianapolis, IN 46256

Order Information
To order more copies of this book or to receive a complete catalog of other products by PDC, contact: **Performance Development Company**
Web Site: www.performancedevelopmentcompany.net
E-Mail: pdc@performancedevelopment.net

Sparks, Linda Raye.
    Business development is everyone's business : a
motivational guide to getting all employees involved /
by Linda Sparks, Kris Butler. -- 1st ed.
    p. cm.
    Includes bibliographical references.
    ISBN: 0-9703266-0-2

    1. Industrial management. 2. Employee motivation.
3. Success in business. 4. Personnel management.
I. Butler, Kris. II. Title.

HF5549.5.M63S63 2000   658.314
                          QBI00-715

Business Development is
Everyone's
Business

Table of Contents

Acknowledgements

The authors wish to extend sincere thanks for the "sincere helpfulness" of those who contributed to this book: Jack Sweeney, Bob Massie, Jack Bainter, Dianne Wyman, Tom DiMartino, John Ferrone, Amy Davidoff, Amy Durosher, Steve Gore, Joan Gore, Butch Buesing, Dan Rothermel, Bruce Kidd, Meg Lambooy, Elaine Voci, Jan Green, Vivian Wright Defrees, Jerry Wilson, Harry Benson, John Barnard, Ron Albright, Evelyn Kelch, Brian Judd, Rick Mendez, David Clegg, Jim Renshaw, Deanna Monroe, Jeff Bennett, George Callahan, Diana Callahan, Judy Carley, Bob Montgomery, Angela Hurley, Chuck Butler, and Jim Sparks.

Business Development is Everyone's Business

Langsenkamp Manufacturing is a Business Development is Everyone's Business organization. Langsenkamp is a company specializing in custom fabrication of aluminum, stainless, and carbon steel for the food processing industry. By design, Langsenkamp is a flat organization that employs few managers and many workers who are encouraged to learn as many job functions as they want. In doing so, employees receive higher pay for mastery and ability. Employees are given opportunities to attend trade shows and customer meetings, making it easy for them to knowledgeably talk with their neighbors and strangers about Langsenkamp. When employees have attended trade shows in the past, they returned to work the next day with new attitudes and perspectives on how they can innovate with the equipment they have.

Langsenkamp builds rapport with customers by sending an engineer and the person who will actually build the equipment to customer meetings. That way, the employee, who is usually tucked away in the plant, gets to know the customer and sees firsthand the application for the equipment. "It pays for itself," says Jack Sweeney, president of Langsenkamp. "Employees come back from a meeting fully understanding what they will be doing rather than simply interpreting the print, thereby reducing the number of errors and increasing customer satisfaction."

Early on, Sweeney invested in business awareness training for all employees and he plans to continue providing the training as new employees join his organization. He also reinvests up to 10% of company profits in the form of quarterly employee bonuses.

"I don't feel like I'm working hard to encourage this behavior," Sweeney says about the successful business development involvement that he's witnessed among his employees. Yet, Business Development is Everyone's Business comes naturally to the employees of Langsenkamp—in fact, they don't even know they're doing it half the time—because when employees get a taste of the thrill of business development and the resulting pride they feel. . .*they are hooked.*

Welcome to the philosophy that Business Development is Everyone's Business.

Just like positive employee morale can be contagious, so can the concept of Business Development is Everyone's Business. Langsenkamp Manufacturing is testimony to the contagiousness of Business Development is Everyone's Business judging by employees' willingness to hand out company literature and develop new products to fit customer needs. Sweeney has also seen the concept spread because of the competitive nature of people. When one employee sees the accolades garnered as a result of bringing in a new business prospect or some useful customer information, naturally the employee wants to join in on the fun.

Throughout this book, we'll come back to Langsenkamp in some of the stories we tell as a way of demonstrating Business Development is Everyone's Business. From this point forward, we will use the acronym **BDEB** (pronounced Bee-Deb) for Business Development is Everyone's Business. Unless you're especially fond of tongue twisters, we have found that BDEB is a phrase that quickly catches on because of its simplicity.

The Business Case for BDEB

What if all your employees worked as hard to promote your company's products and services as your sales and marketing people did? What if the act of developing business for your organization came naturally to employees, spontaneously and without stress? What if you could depend on the fact that all of your employees are your company's best ambassadors, consistently providing excellent customer service and finding additional ways to help customers and co-workers?

When an organization wants to grow and it sets goals for growth, it needs <u>all employees</u>—not just management and sales people—to pull together and work toward one common goal. That's why Business Development is Everyone's Business. Yet, most employees lack the knowledge that is necessary for contributing to business development.

Robert Louis Stevenson once said that everyone sells something. Throughout this book we will demonstrate how you can help all employees, regardless of job role or title, learn how they can provide better customer service, enhance overall reputation for themselves and your company, and support the organization's business goals. We're going to show you the value of educating all employees about your company and communicating company goals and vision. And, we're going to share six BDEB principles that we hope, taken individually, sound like common sense and, considered collectively, present a pleasant and productive business philosophy.

The idea of BDEB is logical and largely based on common sense. Yet, there are some objections, and here are two common ones.

Objection #1

"I can't tell employees that we're making money because if they find out, they'll want more of it!"

The fact of the matter is the more profit the company makes, the more resources that are available to the people in the company. The distribution of these increased resources can take many forms, i.e., bonuses, better working conditions, better equipment with which to do the job, additional training, etc. We believe that organization-wide profit sharing is not an entitlement, but rather appropriate rewards for doing and encouraging more of the activities that increase overall business performance. Profit sharing is a small price to pay considering the long-term benefits of business growth and employee retention.

Objection #2

"We don't have time to do these business development activities because we're too busy trying to sell more stuff!"

What?! The truth is that the more you engage all employees in the act of business development, the less you will have to spend on the act of selling. Plus, you and your employees may already be doing some things that contribute to a BDEB environment. You may just need to direct resources such as time, money, and energy more strategically. Consider an organization where 100% of your employees are having "sales-type" interactions *within the normal framework of their jobs* and the impact it would have on your bottom line. When all employees are leveraging their natural connections, they create awareness about your business.

Research (and book sales!) proves that owners and managers read a lot of business books and professional journals in an attempt to learn about better business practices, innovative management techniques, and strategies for creating and closing more sales. Often, we read to confirm what we already believe. If you are a little skeptical about enlisting the support of **everyone** in your organization for business development, we share this African proverb:

If you think you're too small to make a difference, try going to sleep with a mosquito in the room!

A Definition of Business Development

Business development can mean different things to different companies. Some companies hire a Director of Business Development or Business Development Manager to prospect for new clients and bring about leads in support of the sales function. Other companies hire a business development person to be the salesperson, finding and closing new business. Sometimes people describe business development with words like "stress" and "travel." For most companies, business development activities range from prospecting and relationship building to the act of writing proposals, negotiating, and closing the sale.

We define the concept of business development as the *positive and proactive representation of your organization to everyone with whom you come in contact.* It's how you answer the questions, "So, what do you do?" or "What does your company do?" It's how your company's employees serve both internal and external customers.

David Drennan, in his book, *Transforming Company Culture*, cited one study of customers that showed evidence that a company's employees are often the source of business. People were asked what influenced their buying decisions, and only 2% of the respondents said that their impression of a company came from its advertising. *Thirty percent* of survey respondents said that they knew someone who works or who used to work at that company. Drennan concluded that a company's employees are often their best ambassadors for creating awareness of their products and services in the marketplace.

Consider the valuable connections that are made from a business development standpoint. Do employees form friendships with clients and suppliers that lead to socializing outside of work? Do employees frequently go to lunch with clients, suppliers, and individuals in their respective communities? Do employees run into clients and prospects at the grocery store or at their child's school? Adopting a BDEB attitude simply means that wherever they are and whatever the circumstance, employees must consider themselves as their company's best ambassadors.

You never know when you're going to meet someone who can help grow the business. It could be your next customer, your next employee, or your next referral. Here is one example of how a non-sales employee has the opportunity to make a significant business development connection for his company.

Wearing Many Hats

Business development opportunities present themselves anytime and anyplace. We were with a prospect presenting a proposal for a management training program when we learned that we had a need for *our prospect's* product. The tables turned quickly and the group of managers to whom *we* were presenting quickly began selling *us* on the benefits of their product. *This situation demonstrates that you can be selling even when you are buying!*

It has been said that we use only one-third or less of our brains. Think of trying to run an organization where one-third of the employees contribute to the business development effort and two-thirds sit relatively idle when it comes to business development. What a waste of resources! Contrast that with an organization where *one hundred percent* of employees are engaged in helping develop opportunities to positively impact business.

When 100% of your employees are working to positively and proactively represent themselves and your company to everyone with whom they come in contact, you can begin to build bridges that connect people and processes to make a synergetic effect. People of differing job functions work together toward common business goals, and processes don't restrict creativity and innovation, but rather direct and enhance high performance. When you've got 100% BDEB involvement, your organization has greater potential to become a brand of its own. Employees will naturally create positive awareness of your organization and make valuable connections filled with business development potential. We believe that when all of an organization's employees are making productive connections throughout the natural course of their personal and professional lives, that organization will be more successful as a result.

Every single employee within an organization has the opportunity to contribute to business development by maximizing their connections and daily interactions with customers, family, friends, and fellow employees. Consider the business of news reporting. Journalists must keep current on people and events within their beats, maximizing their connections so they can be successful at getting that next story. So it is in every industry. By connecting with patients at a more personal level, healthcare personnel can help create an atmosphere conducive to high patient satisfaction ratings. Even administrators and teachers in the educational system can and should maximize their connections in the community since people now have more choices as to where they can send their children to school. The overall goal of BDEB is to encourage all employees to consider their world of connections as possible business development opportunities for the achievement of their organization's goals.

Maximizing Your Organization's Connections

The concept of "connections" provides a different view of business development opportunities. It demonstrates that while employees are performing key job functions that appear to be purely project management or administrative, they may, in fact, be performing one of the company's most rewarding business development activities.

Your organization's connections are your link to seeking and finding new business opportunities. Maximizing your organization's natural connections could mean a lot to you if you've ever found yourself wondering, "How can I be more places to sell more?" By encouraging a BDEB culture, you will be able to maximize the natural connections that exist among your *employees* to increase your business development opportunities. Employees can help you *exponentially* increase the number of people who know what your organization does as well as help your organization's *name and image* be more places. As a result, you are more likely to get additional qualified leads.

Instead of reorganizing entirely to start something new, we recommend that you take a good look at your current organization and the typical connections and interactions it has with the rest of the world. This is part of getting a deeper understanding of your organization and inventorying your existing assets. You should identify both formal and informal connections.

In the course of doing business, we believe that employees can be allocated into three primary categories: 1) Getting the work, 2) Doing the work, and 3) Supporting the work.

Primary Employee Function Categories

GETTING the Work	DOING the Work	SUPPORTING the Work
Sales Marketing Advertising Public Relations Management	Project Management Customer Service Project Teams Management	R & D Staff Development Facilities Administration Management
Cost of Sale	Billable	Overhead

Traditional thinking would have us believe that employees who are allocated in the first category are the only employees responsible for business development. But, look at the three categories again. Estimate the number of employees at your company who would be allocated to each of the three categories.

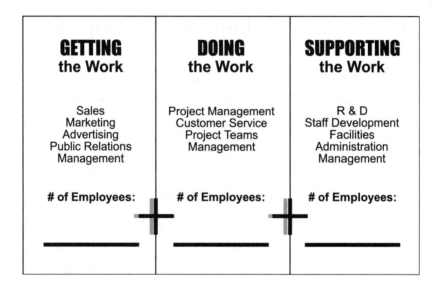

GETTING the Work	DOING the Work	SUPPORTING the Work
Sales Marketing Advertising Public Relations Management	Project Management Customer Service Project Teams Management	R & D Staff Development Facilities Administration Management
# of Employees:	# of Employees:	# of Employees:

How many employees in your organization currently work primarily in the "Getting the work" category? How many employees currently work in the "Doing the work" category? How many employees currently work in the "Supporting the Work" category? Now add them up. Wouldn't it be nice to see 100% of employees contributing in some way to getting the work? Hopefully, you're starting to see the benefits of 100% participation in business development in your organization.

Reaching 100% Employee Participation

There are many ways we can help our employees contribute to business development. This book will walk you through six BDEB principles that are packed with action ideas for helping non-sales and marketing employees practice basic sales and marketing attitudes, skills, and knowledge. For some of you, that's music to your ears! Because, why wouldn't you want all employees working for the common good of the company? Yet, for others, giving all employees the tools and knowledge they need to be business developers is a scary prospect indeed. The key is to make it as natural as possible for non-sales employees to communicate with others inside and outside your company.

Tom Peters, in his book, *Liberation Management,* said that the market demands that each employee be turned into a businessperson. To do that, the organization's information will need to be at everyone's fingertips, which makes some owners and managers uncomfortable. How many of the following excuses do you recognize?

> *"If my employees know about the company's financial position, they*
> *might divulge too much to outsiders."*
> *"I can't trust my employees to make decisions before running them*
> *by me first."*

"If I give them too much information, they might quit and take the information to my competitors."

"I don't think they would really understand the financial details or how we deliver our products/services."

"They don't need to know this information."

For those of you who recognize any of these excuses, we recommend that you work on changing your paradigm. Employees should have access to organizational information and should know the goals of the organization. Rather than simply showing up for a paycheck, employees will be able to take pride in their work and enjoy the success of the business. As a result, they will want to contribute in ways that impact your business development efforts.

One reason why Business Development is Everyone's Business is that it replaces the "not my area" mentality with an "owner" mentality. Giving employees the information and tools they need to make informed decisions on the job frees those in leadership positions to perform those activities for which their expertise is truly needed. And, it provides customers with a greater sense of comfort that they are dealing with people who are truly knowledgeable and helpful.

Helping others improve their business development acumen, though, assumes that they *want* to contribute to business development. Here's an example:

Customer Service Rep or Order Taker?
While at a client's office discussing the development of their
new computer system, I learned of one employee's disgruntle-
ment that the system was taking far too long for a customer
service rep (CSR) to use during a live transaction with a
customer. She explained that it currently takes CSRs one
minute to process an order, and the new system was taking as
much as three minutes just to do a part search! Granted, I
agree that this was too long to wait, but I suggested that those
three minutes could be a good time to get to know the customer a little better and to be a little proactive about finding out
their needs for add-on business. Her response was startling.
She said that, overall, the CSRs at their company didn't want to
get to know the customer. She further explained that the
general perception among CSRs at that company was when
customers think they know you, they ask for special favors.
They believe the way to provide customer service is to take the
call, get the order, and hang up.

So, what's missing from this picture? Perhaps the desire by the employees to truly be of assistance to customers beyond the customers'
immediate expectations. Obviously, CSRs believe that selling add-
on business isn't their job, and they are reluctant to make it their
job. In this particular example, there is a failure by management to
make it a priority that customer service employees get to know their
customers, their businesses, and their future needs. How do your
CSRs think?

John Houghton, Manager of Training at Collision Team of America
says that at their collision repair center there is a sense that to "de-
scend to sales" is to be more like a low cost (and therefore, lower
quality) repair service. But as Houghton puts it, "good sales isn't
about high pressure." It's about planting the seed by suggesting extra things, double checking estimates, and paying attention to customer needs.

Let's not forget that in many instances, your prospective customers have left their homes, driven to your place of business, and are at this very moment asking for your CSRs' professional opinions! Are your CSRs equipped to handle these questions? Do they know that they can significantly influence sales in your organization? Do they have appropriate knowledge and resources to enable them to be effective customer influencers? Pat yourself on the back if you answered "yes" to these questions because your organization is already demonstrating a good foundation for a BDEB culture.

Ode to Business Owners

We need more sales, as profitable sales go.
We need to stabilize our cash flow.
We need to find and retain good staff.
These are the things that we must have!

Six Principles of BDEB

What does your "to-do" list look like? If you are a business owner or manager, chances are you wear many hats—including the sales and marketing sombrero. On your to-do list you probably have responsibility in many different functions including accounting, management, human resources, counseling, training, public relations, marketing, operations, product development, quality control, and proposal/quote preparation, just to name a few.

Consider how the work gets done in your organization. Do you run a manufacturing facility with an assembly line? Does your job description as owner or manager actually include manually working at each station to assemble parts and ship products out the door? No! As an owner or manager, you probably wouldn't assume the responsibility of the employees who deliver the product (unless you had good reason, of course.) So, why would you assume the *business development* responsibility from delivery personnel or other employees, who through routine customer interaction, have opportunities to enhance awareness of your company's other products and services?

BDEB is a practical way to enlist the support of all employees to increase your organization's business success. It is <u>not</u> some hot new trend that will sweep through your company only to be forgotten when the next hot new trend comes along. BDEB isn't a program—it's a philosophy. In fact, it can't be successful as a program, but rather as a new attitude that prevails throughout the company. BDEB is about creating an environment for active listening, thoughtful questioning, and a solid understanding of your business's expertise, which will lead to new sales and solutions to client or prospect problems.

BDEB is not a directive to turn all employees into sales people and "hard-hitting" networkers either. It is a way to encourage employees to positively and proactively represent your company to everyone with whom they come in contact. BDEB is simply getting back to the basics of good business. It comes from an intrinsic frame of mind or attitude--it's common sense. But as it's been said, common sense isn't all that common, especially when it comes to performing those activities that can lead to good customer service or business development.

Business Development is Everyone's Business . . .especially when an organization wants to grow market share, increase customer satisfaction, and gain a competitive advantage. To help accomplish these goals, all employees must understand the six principles of business development and how they can contribute to the company's business development efforts.

BDEB Principles

Principle 1
Maximizing your natural connections with the Five Groups of Influence™ enhances business development.

Principle 2
A constant state of "sincere helpfulness" encourages service quality.

Principle 3
Knowledge of the primary Channels of Opportunity™ can leverage business development resources.

Principle 4
Employees do their best work when they understand how they impact organizational success.

Principle 5
Ongoing staff and work environment development increases organizational potential.

Principle 6
Valuing a variety of business development activities and results improves outcomes.

Putting BDEB Into Action

 **A C T I O N** List three good reasons why you would like to get 100% of your employees involved in business development. Keep this list where you can see it and refer to it often. It will be your motivation as you read this book and implement some of its concepts.

 **A C T I O N** Make a list of all your vendors/suppliers/subcontractors. Build a company profile about them. Include the number of employees, key contact names, a brief description of the services they provide, and the types of customers they serve. Build this list under the assumption that your suppliers could also become your customers and part of your referral network! Assign a task force to determine how your products and services fit with your suppliers' needs and begin the process of communicating to them the benefits of working with you as *their* vendor. There is contact management and database software that automates the process and puts the intellectual capital and contacts in one place. Use it!

 **A C T I O N** Create displays in warehouses, lobbies, and public access corridors that help educate people about the company's products and services.

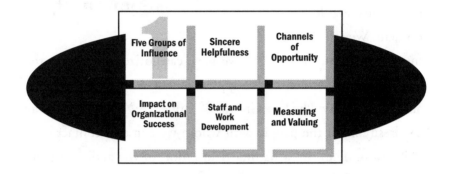

Principle 1

Maximizing your natural connections with the Five Groups of Influence™ enhances business development.

Everyone within the organization, especially employees who are in positions to work with clients, must present themselves and their company in a manner that best represents the organization. As leaders, we must encourage positive representation by demonstrating its importance. We must share with all employees examples of how even one positive employee experience with someone within his Five Groups of Influence™ can have a ripple effect, resulting in an opportunity. We must encourage positive behavior by rewarding positive behavior.

31

The pivotal point of BDEB is taking the moments when you interact with someone and leveraging those events as opportunities for business development. We call these 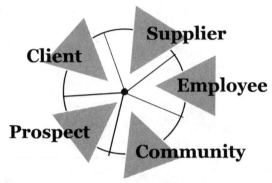 moments "connections," and we have categorized them into the Five Groups of Influence™: Supplier, Client, Employee, Prospect, and Community. The Five Groups of Influence™ are simply a way to classify all of the people with whom we come in contact on a daily basis. They are a natural delineation of the audience types who can influence our business development efforts and are the building blocks of relationships, which are very important to long-term business success.

Everyone within your organization has an opportunity to connect with all Five Groups of Influence™. In fact, if you were to trace how you get new contacts, you'd probably find that you often get them from the existing network of relationships that you've established over time. Many of our company's "business-producing" relationships result from casual contacts—not from formal sales contacts we've pursued or cold calls we've made because we thought they'd be interested in buying our product or service. Doing business is really just working together with a lot of people. It's referred to as business-to-business...yet, it's really just a bunch of people working together—the purchasing director-to-the-sales person...or the customer service representative-to-the-customer...or the consultant-to-the-executive.

Those of us doing business the "personal relationship way" could learn a lot from companies selling products and services over the Internet. E-commerce has become a popular alternative to doing business in person simply because of its ease and transaction efficiency. While customers have minimal expectations that a person-to-person relationship will occur, they are expecting optimal service, product quality, and delivery. And, there is a relationship element to doing business on the Internet: *trust.* In order for people to buy sight unseen, they must trust that they are buying from a legitimate company that intends to sell them something of value. As a result, companies excelling at e-commerce today have a heightened awareness of who they are selling to and what buyers' "hot buttons" are. Sellers are paying extra attention to discovering consumer needs *before* any transaction occurs.

And that's what 100% of your employees should be doing when there are connecting with personal and professional friends, family, and colleagues. Through these natural connections, they could be establishing relationships with people who could tell others about your product or service. In some instances, they could also be learning a great deal about customer and prospect needs.

Are we paying enough attention to the importance of common sense, good relationships, and effective communications? Or, do you find that you are simply following the rules set forth by predecessors under different circumstances? Is your business losing long-term customers by forgetting to nurture relationships?

> **Make New Friends and Keep the Old**
> Here is an example of a long-term relationship that wasn't. The husband of a friend recently applied for a car loan at his bank of over 20 years. He had just started a new job after choosing to stay home for two years to take care of their son while his wife worked. The bank, despite the established relationship and because of their standard operating procedure, turned him down for the loan. He got on the Internet, applied for a car loan through a reputable bank, and received the loan. He has shared this story and his dissatisfaction with his original bank with many friends, family, and business colleagues.

In addition to their job responsibilities, all employees have formal and informal opportunities to connect with customers or prospects. To identify the various and potentially powerful connections that exist for your organization, begin to educate employees about the importance of leveraging their connections for increased business development results. To do this, let's first look at how employees (while doing their core work inside the organization) could potentially connect with all Five Groups of Influence™. We'll take an even closer look at some examples of typical connections within these categories.

The Five Groups of Influence™

Supplier

The Supplier Connection

Our supplier connection is one of the most natural ways we make connections with people. Any individual or organization that provides products or services to your organization is fair game in the quest for business development. The supplier connection includes any organization or independent contractor that is used on client projects, or provides products and services for your organization such as office supplies, uniforms, parts/ materials, legal advice, etc.

In larger organizations, purchasing agents are typically the link to the supplier and have a unique opportunity to develop valuable relationships with salespeople who, themselves, are well connected. Once salespeople from supplier companies know and understand your business, they will be more likely to refer business to you. For example, consider how many of your well-respected vendor's customers could be *your* customers with a suggestion from your vendor to call you!

In addition to vendors, subcontractors or consultants on a temporary assignment are an excellent group to tap into for business development opportunities because when they aren't working on a project, they are typically drumming up business for themselves. Often, these professionals remain close to the pulse of what's happening, and they are quite capable of being additional business development eyes and ears for your organization. They might have advance information on upcoming projects or established relationships to share, giving you an even greater advantage. Subcontractors are professional peers, and you can benefit from routine conversations with them.

Subcontractors Are a Powerful Source of Referrals
Unlike the often negative aspects of responding to Request for Proposals (RFPs,) referrals are a powerful way to get more business . . . especially referrals from subcontractors. We can attest to that. A subcontractor to our company referred one of *his* clients to us for a training project. We won the project, completed the work, and are consistently called back for additional project opportunities.

Look at the list of professional services--including staff recruiters, subcontractors, and vendors--with whom your organization does business. What business development contacts could be made with your accounting and legal firms, bankers, investors, stockholders, commercial laundry service, etc.? These professional suppliers can be excellent leads because they have much to gain from your increased success.

There are two steps to developing business through the supplier connection.

Step 1

Make sure that your suppliers fully understand what your organization does. Many suppliers may not know what you do, or they may have limited knowledge about the extent of your products and services. The more others know about your organization, the better able you are to get more business from referrals. Also, don't underestimate the value of this knowledge for your organization's employee recruitment efforts.

Step 2

Ask your suppliers for their business development support. Never assume that they automatically think of your products and services if given the opportunity to refer business. They should be thanking you for your business and encouraging your referrals on a routine basis—and likewise, you should be thanking them for providing you with good service and encouraging their referrals as well!

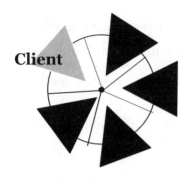

The Client Connection

Your clients represent important connections for your organization's business development efforts. First, you want to keep doing business with repeat clients on a long-term basis. After all, it costs up to six times as much to get a new client than it does to keep one. Second, add-on projects to existing client projects are always welcome. Add-ons are going to happen only when your clients know and understand the breadth of your services and capacity for delivering them. (It also helps if they are satisfied with the services they've received from you to date.)

Your clients can be a distinctive and powerful part of your sales force through word of mouth marketing and referrals. Jerry Wilson, author of the book, *Word-of-Mouth Marketing*, says that the stronger you have made an impression by a combination of factors including service, marketing, reputation, and employees, the more likely you are to get a client's business. Doesn't it follow then that satisfied clients are candidates for referring others to you?

In their book, *Raving Fans*, Ken Blanchard and Sheldon Bowles call the customers who send you referrals your "raving fans." They believe that you shouldn't want to simply provide customer satisfaction, but rather service that creates clients who sing your praises to everyone—who are "wildly excited" about your products and services! Clients want to be able to confidently refer your organization to others, and for someone to refer your business, they must know someone *and* have confidence that your company can help the "referred" party. After all, no one wants to look bad by sending business to a company that ultimately doesn't deliver.

Project managers have tremendous influence with the client connection. In addition to project-related contact with clients, project managers and other project team members should have opportunity-focused contact. What this means is that at all times during the project, these employees should be listening for ways in which your organization can provide value-added products and services. Opportunity-focused contact builds an infrastructure to support and encourage the development of expanded relationships, which could result in expanded contracts!

Nurturing Repeat Business

One information technology (IT) consulting firm's success lies in its ability to win lucrative project work from existing clients in the form of "add-on" contracts. These add-ons can be actual project expansions or new projects that are "disguised" as add-on work to an existing contract. Since the longevity of projects is typically as much as two years, more opportunity-focused contact by project managers would strengthen relationships and lead to additional business. Since this firm's project employees do the bulk of their project work while being housed in the client's offices, they are at the pulse of their client's spoken and unspoken needs. Clearly, as long as their goal is to focus on opportunities to provide top-notch service and watch for ways to add value, add on projects will follow.

Wide and deep is the goal here. When you take time to consider the lifetime value of a client you can justify investing more of your organizational resources in broadening the relationship. Think of your personal buying habits for a moment. When you buy consumer products such as cars, air conditioning units, appliances--big ticket items--you go back again and again to the same supplier who you trust. It is this same trust that you want 100% of your employees to establish in their daily interactions with their Five Groups of Influence™, especially clients.

Examine the primary activities your organization does to connect with clients. For example, when they first became a customer, how did you welcome them? How do you communicate project and/or account status and general news about your company to them? How do you bill them for your products and services? How do you manage their expectations? Do you call on them when you aren't trying to sell something? Do you send them notes of congratulations when you hear good news about them?

Remember, you and your employees are the experts at what you do. You have a responsibility to keep clients calm, informed, and feeling confident that they made the right choice in your company. James McEachern, Chairman of the Board and CEO of Tom James Company says, "If a buyer has confidence in you, your company, and your product, making the sale becomes a piece of cake." If the only time you talk with your client is when there is a problem or a decision to be made, you miss out on the opportunities for the small talk that yields referrals and positive feedback for your organization. This is when the strength of numbers—100% employee involvement—plays an important factor in your organization's ability to develop additional business opportunities.

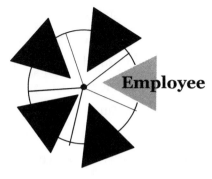

The Employee Connection

There are two types of customers: external and internal. Since we've already discussed how you can leverage your existing relationships with your customers to develop more business, let's now explore how you can develop business by leveraging the talents and knowledge of your internal customers—employees.

How employees communicate to each other about the work they do has tremendous influence on your business development activities. For example, it's the salesperson who gets the credit for a sale even though others in the organization, such as administrative assistants, engineers, and proposal writers had a hand in the effort. The sales person who presents the proposal to the client is in the best position to tell the other contributors how the client reacted to the proposal's contents. What worked in the proposal and what didn't work? Employees whose jobs are to help write proposals are often the last people to receive the very information that can help them do a better job on the next proposal.

Proposals That Get the Order

We have presented proposals that were written by our proposal writer with such on-target customer-specific information that the decision to hire us was made during the presentation. We brought this information back to her and applauded her efforts, allowing her to celebrate the win along with us.

Since sales people are on the front line with customers, they have a huge opportunity to share what they know about customers and help employees understand how what they do provides customer satisfaction. Who else is on the front line with customers in your organization? Service technicians, for example, can provide information to the sales rep on how customers use the products his company sells. He can bring insight on how businesses use certain pieces of equipment and tell engineers and sales people why and how equipment fails. This information will help the organization improve product development and product sales.

For employees, the positive and proactive representation of your company is a critical business development activity. Are *your* employees positively and proactively representing themselves and your organization to everyone with whom they come in contact? Do they know the value of doing this? Do they know *how to* positively and proactively represent their organization to their connections? You might be surprised at what you find out if you were to ask these questions.

It's All Relative

In spite of encouraging employees to bring business leads to the marketing department, one construction firm experienced frustration that its employees still weren't complying. The problem became painfully obvious when one of the firm's superintendents told the marketing director that his sister's company was planning to build a new building. After checking on the status of the project, the superintendent learned that the project had already been awarded to one of its competitors *in spite of the fact that the superintendent's sister was a decision-maker at her company.*

What happened here? Clearly, the superintendent's sister didn't think to ask her brother for advice on the building project nor did she invite his company to bid. Do your friends and family truly understand what products and services your company provides? Do they know you are interested in new opportunities to serve? Don't put yourself or your employees in the position to agonize over a deal your company should have had. Teach your employees to value their connections by sharing what they do in a non-threatening, yet exuberant way with their family and friends.

Here is a positive story about an employee who uncovered important information that contributed to add-on business for his company.

BDEB Happens Anytime, Anyplace

The customer service manager for a bearing and chain manufacturing company lived next door to a man who works for one of its largest customers. One day as he was enjoying a neighborly visit with this man, the customer service manager learned of a new business opportunity for his company. He immediately sent this information to a sales person and requested a quick follow-up with the customer. He recognized that while it wasn't his job to close the sale, it was his job to influence it by asking permission to have a salesperson follow-up with the appropriate individual at his neighbor's company.

Don't discount the power that internal employee relationships bring to your marketing efforts. Various employee groups have unique perspectives and insights about the business. Capitalize on this knowledge by encouraging an environment of cross-functional awareness. Many companies do this by creating cross-functional teams that meet regularly to discuss client projects with the intent to develop better understanding of client needs, company expertise, and prospective new work. Companies that regularly hold company picnics and employee get-togethers know how important it is to nurture strong employee relationships across departmental divides. The more employees know and trust each other, the more likely they are to collaborate on projects, help out when help is needed, and refer your organization to potential recruits. As long as camaraderie exists, employees who leave your organization for whatever reason will likely continue to make positive connections for the organization.

Goodbye Isn't Always Good Riddance

Before one of Langsenkamp's employees left for another job that was closer in proximity to his home, he asked a project engineer to quote on a piece of work for his new company. The employee had told his new employer about Langsenkamp's capabilities, who, in turn, provided him with a handful of prints for the parts they needed.

The overall philosophy at Langsenkamp is that "if you work here, you contribute to sales." As a result of the company's commitment to sharing information with all employees regardless of position, more employees are contributing directly to the bottom line.

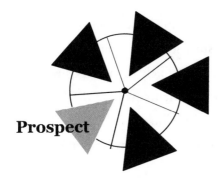

Prospect

The Prospect Connection

We define prospects as those companies that have a defined project and the potential for a request for proposal in the works. Prospects are buyers who know who you are and agree that your products and services may fit their needs. Prospects are also those companies or individuals that you know are actually buying your specific product or service. They have either expressed an interest in working with you directly or through a third party. Prospects fit the description of your ideal customer and you either call on them, or they call you.

When a prospect has been identified, they are often considered a "fragile" contact since their opinion of your organization could be positive or negative depending on the interaction. That's why many owners and managers take the posture of protectiveness and limit the exposure that prospects have with certain employee groups to reduce the risk of someone saying the wrong thing. These protective managers doubt that some employees can be *positive* opinion molders, believing instead that certain employees are a poor representation of their organization. (By their refusal to involve them, they imply that it's best to keep these folks in the back room where no one sees them!)

The point is, prospect connections happen—sometimes by design, sometimes by chance. The best way to benefit from (or survive) them is to learn to recognize and leverage them. When owners and managers take time to properly train employees, giving them guide-lines for expected behaviors and sufficient information about their company, these employees will be more likely to make positive con-nections with prospects. Prospective clients will see that there are several individuals at the organization who are knowledgeable and helpful, and, as a result, the prospects will have a better overall image of the company.

Clients Can Be Prospects, Too

Here is an example of how employees who actually do the work have the opportunity to turn a customer into a prospect for another division in their company. In the design industry, for example, architects, engineers, and interior designers are some-times contracted by real estate developers or building contractors for a specific piece of an overall design project. If an architectural firm is hired to design a building exterior, there is no reason why the interior designers in the firm shouldn't have a chance to quote on the potentially lucrative interior design work. Another example is when space planners are contracted by a real estate developer to lay out the space for a building tenant. These designers have a tremendous opportunity to influence the building tenant's selec-tion of interior design firms simply because they get to know the needs of the company during their plan of the new space.

Do you have an organization where a group of employees working in one division has the opportunity to influence business develop-ment for another division? A prospect can materialize when two things occur: 1) An employee takes the time to show an interest in the prospect's business, and 2) the employee knows enough about all divisions of his company to be able to create enough interest by the prospect for more information. This is a good example of why cross-functional awareness among employee groups is so important for business development success.

Community

The Community Connection

The community connection is everyone around you who doesn't already fit into one of the other four groups of influence. They are connected with you at Little League games, the grocery store, the parent-teacher organizations, local social and service clubs, and industry-specific conferences, to name a few. This group also includes members of your family and anyone who may someday need a product or service you can provide, but at the present time has no need or interest. Community is often the least recognized area of influence though it can sometimes contain the highest level of natural connections. Here is an example that illustrates what a small world this is and how our natural community connections support BDEB:

It Really is a Small World, After All

I recently reconnected after several years with a friend of mine who is the marketing director for a large building contractor. I called him after my husband mentioned he'd run into him at a committee meeting they both attended for an outside organization. During our visit, my friend and I swapped stories about our lives since we last talked and the ages of our children. At the mention of my son's school, my friend said that he was on the school board in that township. I told him that my husband and I really liked the school and especially liked my son's teacher. My friend asked who the teacher was. I told him, and then he said that she is his neighbor. Then he said she is the wife of another mutual friend of ours with whom I'd been meaning to reconnect for business and personal reasons.

How many connections do you see in this true story that took place in a city of approximately one million people? Multiply connections such as these—because we all have them—with 100% of your employees, and you can see how community connections can be valuable business development contributions if considered in the appropriate context. It is the connections we make that turn what could be considered "cold calls" into warm leads for new business development.

Encouraging your employees to leverage their natural connections can be compared to a plant whose root system spreads out over a wider diameter than its above-ground vegetation. The better and more dense the root system, the more likely the plant will survive

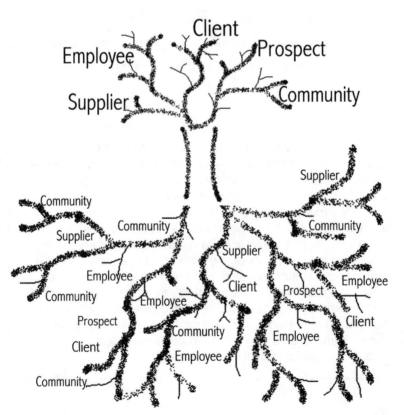

and prosper. The same could be said for your organization. What might be the benefits and opportunities for your organization of connecting more deliberately with the community? One benefit might be to strengthen the opportunity for a successful prospecting call. Another might be to strengthen the awareness of your products and services to people who know you, but not your company. Yet another might be to establish a communications "root system" in support of your marketing plan.

One way for employees to become more involved in the community is to volunteer their time on meaningful activities such as charities and not-for-profits, trade and/or professional association committees or boards, special city events that appreciate corporate involvement, and neighborhood initiatives. Some employees might choose to become involved in the arts, church, or in politics. Encourage their active participation. Your goal is to help them understand that their involvement also serves as a valuable business development activity and that their level of involvement and commitment is how others will view them *and* your organization. (It may be useful to provide time management guidelines for committee involvement so employees don't get sidetracked from or lose sight of the goals and responsibilities of their regular work activities!)

Making Confident Employees

Your employees' confidence in how well they know the company is the key to their ability to have a productive conversation with people in their Five Groups of Influence™. Knowledge is truly power, and it is the critical link for employees and the customers they serve. You can see evidence of this in the grocery store checkout line when a new clerk is learning how to do his/her job. Have you ever wanted to move to a different line when you see a new clerk in training? Perhaps you don't want the clerk learning on your time? The clerk is usually intimidated by the whole thing as well, worried about forgetting an important step or messing up a sale and having to start all over again. Their anxiety is contagious and as a result, it often takes longer to conduct a transaction.

It begins the same way each time someone new trains for a position within your organization. Customers and employees who ask questions of the new employee are met with blank stares, frightened looks, and answers of "I don't know, I'm new here." But ask that employee a question six months later, and you'll find a totally different employee. And, once an employee who is truly customer-focused knows the basics of his job, he has greater confidence to try new things to provide better customer service.

Research shows that in selling situations it takes up to seven mean-ingful contacts with a prospect to gain their business. Compare that to advertising. It takes up to *24 exposures* to your advertising mes-sage for consumers to remember your product or service. When all employees are confident, they can leverage their natural connec-tions and create awareness about your business to everyone with whom they come in contact. This extra employee effort supports your investment in advertising, making the likelihood of a positive business development return that much higher.

Developing Your Own Information Bite

There are several ways you can help your employees be more confi-dent, more proactive, and positive in their representation of them-selves and your organization. One of the best ways is to teach all employees your organization's information bite--a sound bite that briefly summarizes a company in laymen's terms.

How well do you know your organization? How well can you sum-marize your organization's products and services into a brief infor-mation bite? Let's find out. Read each of the nine questions and answer them (briefly) with the knowledge that you currently pos-sess about your company.

1. What is the name of your organization?
2. What does the organization do?
3. How many years has the organization been in business?
4. How many employees does it have?
5. What kinds of products or services does it sell?

6. Name your organization's unique niche or product line.

7. Who are the organization's customers?

8. What does customer service mean to the organization?

9. How does the organization currently support sales or business development?

Were you *comfortably* able to answer *all* of the questions? Now let's create your information bite. You don't have to use all of the information contained in all nine questions. Remember that this description of your company is a brief, yet versatile message. Imagine using it at your daughter's soccer game or in the grocery store checkout line. In your own words, write a <u>brief</u> information bite in answer to the following question: Who do you work for and what does your company do?

As you can see, it can be difficult to succinctly answer what you do within one or two sentences. Brevity can be crucial especially during a first contact with someone. Stephen Covey calls this information bite an "elevator speech" because you often have less than a minute to answer a question or tell a person something on an elevator. It is common for people to feel uncomfortable with their information bite because they're not sure they're covering everything that needs to be said about their organization. They feel they can't write an information bite about their company because it is just too darn multi-faceted. Or, they think that before they can even answer the questions, they must first evaluate who is asking and then tailor their answer based on the person's level of experience or knowledge. Actually, the information bite works because it is universal, not because it is targeted to an individual market.

If you're uncomfortable creating an information bite, how do you think your employees feel when faced with answering the question, "What do you do?" Every single employee in your organization should be able to comfortably and confidently answer the "What do you do?" question because it's inevitable--they will be asked this question sometime. (In fact, Dale Carnegie teaches people to use this question as a conversation starter for effective networking.) When the question is answered well, the result is a form of unpaid advertising for your company. Having a well-prepared answer also confirms their understanding and knowledge of the big picture of your organization.

Employees who aren't happy in their work probably won't tell anybody anything about it. As a former turnaround consultant for many struggling companies, Jack Sweeney found that when employees have high job satisfaction and trust where they work, they are more likely to tell more people about their company. For example, at Langsenkamp, Sweeney employs several people whose hobbies include automobile swap meets. These employees have ample opportunity to meet other car enthusiasts at these events who are also decision makers in their own companies. Sweeney's employees tell him that the question, "Where do you work?" always comes up, and they make sure they're prepared with a quick answer.

Selling services requires that the person doing the selling can communicate what kind of service it is. But what about the employee who works as a systems analyst in a company that sells information technology and consulting services? Can he effectively communicate what your company does when asked by his second cousin at next weekend's family reunion? While an accounts payable clerk doesn't need to fully understand the complex formula for your company's specialty fruit juice, she should understand its unique difference from the competitors, how it tastes, and why it's good for you! After all, she is a customer as well as an employee. Her influence on others around her will encourage them to purchase your product.

Product sales are an easy example. Your company makes toilet paper? I buy toilet paper! Your company makes garage doors? My garage door is on its last leg. Your company sells recreation sets? My cousin wants to purchase a recreation set for her six-year-old. Thinking about buying a new dishwasher? Look no further—my friend works at a small family-owned appliance store. Installation is free and service is guaranteed! See how easy it is to make these connections? Again, *Business Development Is Everyone's Business!*

The better you and your employees are at succinctly describing what you do, the more likely your *customers* are to understand your business and tell their professional peers about you. Rather than hearing your customer say, "They are our supplier for custom widgets," you might hear them say, "Their company is a supplier to the automotive industry and manufactures parts for plastic consoles, doors, and other interior accessories." Or, how about this one: Instead of, "They do our advertising," you might hear your client say, "They are an ad agency that specializes in designing strategic promotional campaigns based on any marketing budget. They're very creative and do print and broadcast media, brochures, annual reports, corporate identity campaigns, and web site design. I'd highly recommend them for your business!" And, when you can get your customers into the act of developing business for your company, you're well on your way to business prosperity!

Other than the use of the information bite, what are some other ways in which your non-sales employees can help you win more business from clients and prospects? Referrals and word-of-mouth marketing is a powerful way to sell products and services, especially if your employees are users of your products.

When all employees maximize their natural connections with the Five Groups of Influence™, they can enhance your organization's business development efforts significantly. Armed with knowledge and a positive attitude, employees will be confident in their ability to battle the competition by positively and proactively representing their company to everyone with whom they come in contact.

Speaking from Experience

A friend of ours participated in a marketing survey examining the services of executive physical exam programs in Central Indiana. When she called Ball Memorial Hospital, she got the receptionist. The receptionist was not the contact person for the program, nor was she a salesperson by job definition. Her job was simply to direct inquiries. Our friend explained what she was after and the receptionist gave her the name and number of the person at Ball Memorial to contact. But then the receptionist did a remarkable thing. She also went on to tell our friend that she, herself, had been through Ball's program, having chosen it for the cost benefit, and that it was wonderful. She spoke about the program in detail, stressing its professionalism and commitment to the individual.

On this particular survey, our friend wrote, "This is the program to beat – not because of the program itself, but because of this receptionist who naturally markets what she believes in with a high degree of conviction." This receptionist had naturally discovered the key to enhancing customer relationships through her knowledge of the program and her honest enthusiasm and appreciation of its merits. About a year later our friend learned that the receptionist had been promoted to Assistant Marketing Director. Management had recognized her efforts.

Putting Principle 1 Into Action

ACTION

Educate all employees on the types of products and services your company provides. Consider the following information in the development of an orientation program:

• History of company

• Company income history and financial picture

• Mission, vision, and goals

• Sales and marketing strategies

• Who your competitors and clients are

• Your clients' businesses and market factors

• What and why your clients buy from you

Taking It Professionally

When Rodney, a welder at Langsenkamp, was invited by his girlfriend to attend her company-sponsored supervisory dinner, he realized that his girlfriend's company might be important to Langsenkamp's business. Sure enough, Rodney learned that the company was a current prospect and that Langsenkamp had even submitted a quote on a large piece of business with them. He prepared for the evening by learning as much about the nature of the proposal and other pertinent facts. The evening of the event, Rodney not only attended; he and his girlfriend sat at the president's table, and together, they spent the evening talking about Langsenkamp! The story has a happy ending as well. Langsenkamp later won the business.

Include all employees in your story! Remember listening to your mother or father as they told you funny or poignant stories about your childhood? People love a story, especially if it involves the birth of a company, and when you personalize your message, employees remember it better.

Provide all employees with copies of your company's marketing and product literature. Not only that, instruct them to keep copies within reach for easy retrieval. Encourage them to give their copies to clients and friends when appropriate. And, be sure to replace their supply when they give their copies away. Encourage employees to keep a record of to whom they give company literature to help you track your Channels of Opportunity™ should any of these people become buyers of your products or services.

Regardless of title, give every single employee a business card, and encourage employees to hand their cards out often. Business cards are a source of pride for employees. Business cards are like phone books. Remember Steve Martin in the movie, *The Jerk*, yelling: "The new phone books are in, the new phone books are in. . .I am somebody!" They are proof of employees' identity with your company, but more importantly, they are 3 ½" x 2" highly transportable advertisements that are fairly inexpensive compared to the costs of display ads and broadcast media. Business cards are a tremendous marketing investment displaying your company's logo, address, and phone numbers for everyone whose hands that card falls into. Business cards are employees' portable notebooks where they write information to give to others. "Give me a call, my home number is on the back," says the employee to the plumber. Yes, and *your* number is on the front!!!

ACTION Tell employees who an ideal customer is for your business. Give them the profile of your current customers. Many employees do not know this information and will appreciate knowing it. Share your organization's Channels of Opportunity™ with employees.

ACTION Make sure that employees have a complete list of all employees' names, departments, titles, and extension numbers. Have you ever called a company only to be transferred to several different departments in search of the appropriate person to help you? Giving your employees a complete internal directory eliminates confusion should a call be transferred to the wrong person. Or, perhaps the customer selects the wrong department after listening to an automated direct line directory. A corporate directory also enables employees to have quick access to co-workers in different departments, thereby further supporting the employee connection.

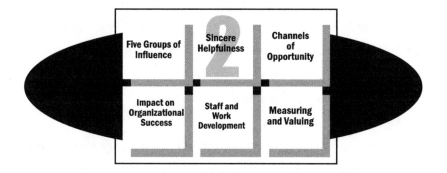

Principle 2

A constant state of "sincere helpfulness" encourages service quality.

The principle of "sincere helpfulness" begins with the intrinsic desire to help others. A "helping organization" is one where employees, regardless of their position, exemplify a genuine desire to help people within their Five Groups of Influence™. Qualities of a sincerely helpful individual are eagerness, enthusiasm, earnestness, and honesty. Other qualities are listening actively and demonstrating courtesy, respect, and concern, responding non-defensively, taking the initiative to satisfy customers and create winning solutions, and helping customers maintain their self-esteem.

Employees who are genuinely glad to be helping others show it with their pleasant and friendly attitude. Witness a friend of ours who uses a mirror on the wall by her phone to remember to smile during phone calls. Not only can you "hear" her smile over the phone, her whole demeanor is one of pleasantness and sincerity. This same friend bought a book at a yard sale for a professional colleague because the book related to her colleague's business. She sent the book with a note that said, "I thought of you when I saw this book. Enjoy!" Sincere helpfulness is demonstrated each time an employee sends an article or recommends a web site to someone, knowing he would find it useful.

That is not to say that only those individuals who are *pleasant* and *friendly* are sincerely helpful. Certainly those qualities contribute to an atmosphere of sincerity and altruism. Employees can be sincerely helpful in ways other than being perceived as pleasant or friendly. Employees who naturally "go the extra mile" to help others when they could use some help, themselves, might actually have more of a grimace on their face from a heavy workload. Yet, they choose to set aside time to help others and not complain about it. There is the employee who gruffly, but *willingly*, lends a hand as the resident computer guru, for example. In spite of the gruffness, which is probably a personality trait, he puts out there that he is sincere about using his talent on the computer to help others do their jobs better. And, don't forget the in-house subject matter expert on a specific technology who lends her ideas and expertise on a proposal. In spite of having a demanding job to do, she takes time to add suggestions for the approach that wouldn't have been there other-wise.

The principle of being sincerely helpful is just that—being helpful *and* sincere about it—not doing something because someone told you to do it or because you'll get a reward after it's finished. While you can't force people to be sincerely helpful, you can demonstrate its importance and show them how they might benefit from it. One of the biggest benefits of sincerely helping others is that you get a chance to learn from other people. When what you're giving is your time and your willingness to listen, you end up learning about people's jobs and work issues as well as what's important to people. Dale Carnegie said that helping others gives you "something priceless"—a feeling that you have done something for someone without expecting anything in return. Using your talent, ideas, and experience to help others is one of the noblest endeavors a person can do. Helping others gives very real business rewards as well. "Help given freely and sincerely can generate the kind of loyalty that is the goal of relationship marketing," said Ford Harding in the book, *Rain Making*. And, that's what BDEB is all about: 100% of your organization's employees building relationships with their connections in an effort to create business development opportunities.

Based on their attitudes at any given time, people in an organization have the ability to positively enhance or negatively affect a customer relationship. Think back to a time when you witnessed a conflict of an organization's values and the attitudes and behaviors of its employees. Perhaps the company boasted that it values people; yet, when you called the company, you were transferred through the voice mail system, never speaking to a live person. Is this company truly valuing people? The goal of being sincerely helpful is to create an expectation that people within your Five Groups of Influence™ can go to you for assistance and advice when needed. Just think of the benefits to your organization if 100% of your employees are willing helpers in all of their work and volunteer activities, and they consistently present this image to the public.

Consider the following three key activity categories to encourage the practice of sincere helpfulness:

1. Adopting a host mentality
2. Sharing what you can with others
3. Promoting referability

Adopt a Host Mentality

Adopting a host mentality changes the perspective from a person who expects to be waited on to someone who does the serving or hosting. It positions you to be considered in positive terms by others as "reliable," "helpful," and "considerate." Each employee's personal dependability will be an example for the entire organization as long as he is consistent and sincere about helping others.

Hosting is a form of receiving guests and visitors into your space, whether it is your corporate offices or your personal space such as an individual office or area in which you're standing. When employees adopt a host mentality, they are always ready to ask if they can help someone in any way. Visitors to your company should be greeted with "May I get you something to drink?" or "May I take your coat?" regardless of the position of the employee. It says a lot for your organization if your guest must decline the offer of assistance from several people rather than to have never been asked throughout his visit. Receptionists' primary responsibility is to act as host to people visiting your organization, and they often ask, "May I help you?" as soon as someone walks in the door. Conversely, you know you're not welcome when the receptionist acts "put out" that her work has been interrupted by your arrival. Some organizations prepare their receptionists for visitors by giving them a list of people who are expected to arrive throughout the day. But, it is also the receptionist's job to be courteous to people who aren't expected even if the receptionist must turn away the caller.

Worth Every Penny

Within the first five minutes that visitors step into the lobby at CSO Architects Engineers & Interiors, Jane Mullin, the receptionist, establishes an excellent first impression of CSO. Jane's important contributions as the first person people see when they walk in the door has been widely recognized as a component of the company's success by both the industry and her company. "Jane spends time getting to know people and establishing a common ground," said Denise Nelson, CSO's Director of Human Resources. She makes everyone feel important whether they are customers or suppliers, and she remembers all names. Jane sets an excellent example of how others in the organization should think and behave when presented with the opportunity to meet and mingle with prospective customers. Her tenure with the company supports the notion that she is truly valued by management and rewarded for the positive influence she has had over the years with the company on business development and retention.

Everyone in an organization can be a host. Hosting within the realm of your personal space means encouraging others to join in on your conversation at a public event, for example. A proper host always makes introductions, and when necessary, introduces himself first to make the newcomer feel comfortable. All project employees who work at the client's office should be hosts and never expect others to wait on them. They should get their own coffee, and while they're at it, fill others' cups as well! Employees who visit their clients' offices regularly should make their own copies during meeting breaks, and show a sincere desire to help at the meeting if others are involved.

When you attend any type of meeting or special event, make your attendance at the event work for you and your organization by adopting a hosting mentality. Don't just plant yourself at a table and wait for the meeting to begin. Adopt the attitude that there is a pretty good chance that there are people at the meeting with whom you have something in common. So get up, meet people, and enjoy yourself. If you see someone who looks busy, consider asking him if he would like some help. Chances are there is something you can do such as placing handouts at each table setting, and as a bonus, you've just made a valuable connection with the meeting host or possibly the speaker.

Another way to be a host is to make valuable connections between people at meetings you attend. For example, if during your conversation with John Smith, the banker, your friend, Mary Jones, the business owner, walks up to say hello. The act of "hosting" is a way in which you can introduce people you know to others to help them make a mutually productive connection.

Share What You Can

Encourage employees to eagerly share their own subject matter expertise for the purpose of educating others and to be recognized as a resource for clients, suppliers, and business partners. Letting people know that they can call you and receive "free and timely information" will result in more business opportunities for your organization. If your organization employs 100 people, that's 100 conduits of resource sharing that can result in significant business development opportunities.

Sharing what you can with others is one of the easiest things to do when it comes to serving clients and friends. You will be seen as someone who knows things, someone who others want to be around. The result is that you will have the chance to have that second conversation, thereby giving you the opportunity to strengthen that connection. Be perceived as the "go to" person. You know you're doing this well when you begin meeting people who have heard of you and are pleased to finally get to meet you in person! Robert Montgomery, CEO of Montgomery Zukerman & Davis calls this "dressing well." He says, "It's not a Rolex watch and a clean shirt but rather 25 words that you want people to say about you when you're not there."

What can you share with others? Do you have an often-unused meeting space that you can share with clients and suppliers? Are you the one in the family with a pick-up truck, and if so, do you frequently (and willingly) help others move? Would others describe you as someone who'd gladly give the shirt off his back to someone? Keep in mind that the principle of sincere helpfulness does not mean that you always have to give information out for free, especially if what you do for a living makes you an easy target for free advice. Don't allow others to misuse you for what you can give them but rather have a plan for those inevitable questions. It is helpful for you to know what kind of information you can give out easily and when it is time to suggest a professional relationship or more formal arrangement.

Sharing what you can is an effective channel for business development since people will be calling you and your employees for information. Your ability to answer their questions and show interest in their subject will result in more business. Jennifer Hobbes, Director of Marketing at Schenkel Schultz Architects, calls the act of sincerely helping customers and friends "passive-solar marketing" because of its powerful outcomes. She has spent extra time at clients' offices simply helping them communicate with technical vendors on such things like installing electrical outlets and phone jacks. Stephen Covey refers to this level of helpfulness as making deposits into emotional bank accounts.

When and where are your opportunities to be sincerely helpful within your Five Groups of Influence™? Consider the following list and check how each idea might apply to opportunities to share what you can within the Five Groups of Influence™.

Opportunities for Sharing	Five Groups of Influence				
	Suppliers	Clients	Employees	Prospects	Community
Information from magazines, books, and newsletters					
Meeting rooms					
Our time in support of their goals					
Resources such as corporate library, document templates, organization and/or facilitation skills					
New business referrals or potential employees					
Lessons learned					
Professional expertise					
Transportation					
Invite people to attend industry meetings and trade shows					
Bring menus back from area restaurants					
Keep reproducible copies of relevant information and news					

Now, customize your own list. Gather good ideas for your list by reviewing comments from satisfied clients and brainstorming with employees.

> **While I've Got You On The Phone. . .**
> The phone rang early one Tuesday morning. It was the plant
> supervisor at a new manufacturing facility on the south side of
> town. The executive director of the local training association
> referred him to us as the firm to call for training resources.
> During the call, we answered his questions, referred him to an
> expert on the subject about which he was inquiring, and showed
> a genuine interest in his project by asking him questions and
> encouraging him to think of alternative workforce development
> methods. Toward the end of the call, he said, "By the way, do
> you do...?" The answer was yes. We got the business. Chalk
> one up for sincere helpfulness.

Networking is a prime opportunity to demonstrate your attitude of
sincere helpfulness. Knowing the type of individuals who will likely
be at an event will help you plan what kinds of information you can
bring to the table. Let's say that the publications you routinely read
provide useful data supporting high performance work teams. Men-
tioning this information in the context of your conversation with a
manager might inspire her to request more information on the topic.
Tell her that you can send a copy of the article and then ask if she
would like to be included on your mailing list for future mailings.

The key concepts of effective networking are:
- Possessing more of a resource mentality by having more con-
  cern for giving than receiving
- Routinely reading trade magazines, news, and anything others
  might like to discuss or need to know
- Knowing what you are uniquely qualified to contribute or give
- Anticipating some requests for information or advice
- Following through with what you say you will do

Promote Referability

Many businesses depend on referrals over other forms of promotion for the growth of their organization. Law firms and physician practices receive a large chunk of their business through referrals. The same could be said for hair stylists, massage therapists, and home remodeling contractors, to name a few. And, some people simply won't do business with companies unless they have been referred by a friend or respected business associate. This is further demonstrated by the success of companies that have been formed strictly to produce referral-based service directories such as Angie's List, a national referral service directory company.

Referrals are the result of on-going, mutually satisfying relationships, and many things will impact you and your organization's referability. For example, you may not have considered advertising in your local trade and professional journals as a valuable business development channel for your company. But, if you study where your business comes from and find that referrals from this network are an important opportunity channel, then maybe you can view these advertising opportunities differently.

There are several channels of "referability" that you must consider: clients, professional/trade/industry peers, business community peers, and suppliers. How many different client contacts referred you? A mistake that many people make is assuming that these valuable referral groups know enough of what your organization does to be able to communicate it to others. For example, many of your customers could have a small frame of reference regarding your company if they only buy one or two things from you. To ensure that your organization can benefit from referral marketing, make sure these customers know exactly what your company does and all of the products and services it provides. You can do this in many ways by:

- Sending routine informational mailings to contacts
- Sponsoring occasional open houses
- Taking time to establish genuine one-to-one relationships with key contacts at your client companies to get to know their business needs better

You can't buy referrals. But an attitude of sincere helpfulness can increase the confidence that others have in you and your employees. This should further support the desire for 100% positive and proactive representation of your organization to everyone with whom employees come in contact.

The Awesome Power of Negative Referrals

During lunch at an industry association meeting, an exchange had taken place at the table that involved two company owners discussing a supplier for a specialized manufacturing process. One owner asked the other for his recommendation of a company that could provide a specialty service they needed for an important project. The other owner suggested a company, which prompted a negative reaction. In fact, the guy had gone on and on in front of the others at the table about why he would *not* want to do business with this company. He'd experienced the service from that company, he said, and while they were experts at the process, he refused to work with them again because their people were slow to respond and acted like they didn't care about his business.

Technical Assistance Research Programs, Inc. published data that showed: For each negative experience a customer has with a company, it takes an average of 12 positive experiences to offset the negative one. For every complaint made by a customer there are 25 other unspoken complaints. And what happens if the matter isn't resolved? People with a complaint against a company tend to tell an average of 10 other people about it.

Isn't referability one of the ultimate measures of success? What a compliment to your business when a satisfied someone inside or outside a company refers you to a friend or business acquaintance!

Obviously "buzz" works. So, how can *you* create positive buzz to promote referability for your company?

Creating Buzz

The bumblebee can be heard from a distance as it approaches its sweet smelling target. What makes a creature as small as a bumblebee heard over the din of traffic and other noise? It's the buzz! Creating positive buzz has been the talk of Hollywood for decades and now the business world has jumped on the bandwagon, realizing that "buzz" marketing is a great way to get the business you seek. Miramax, the studio that produced the movies, *Good Will Hunting* and *Shakespeare in Love*, has practically written the book on creating buzz that wins the gold.

For example, during Oscar time, studios must abide by certain rules. Employees who work in any of the studios with nominated movies are not allowed to call any of the Academy members directly. Miramax, on the other hand, has been creative, having its employees talk with *friends* of the voters, telling two people about how great the movie is, who tell two people, who tell two people, and so on. This, along with a powerful advertising and publicity campaign, has given Miramax the reputation as the studio to beat in the competition for the prize.

Sincere Helpfulness and Customer Service

Every person in your organization views things from a different perspective, given their unique point of contact. But, each employee will have an impact, good or bad, through their interaction with a customer, based on their job function, their knowledge of the company, and even their belief systems.

Just in Customer Service

Before I purchased my home computer, I walked into a large computer store in Indianapolis with the intent to buy. When 20 minutes had gone by and I still had not been approached by a salesperson, in spite of seeing some of them on the floor, I walked in the direction of the customer service desk to ask for help. On my way, I saw a store employee walking toward me, and as she drew near, she averted her eyes, signaling to me, "Don't bother me, don't ask me questions, get away!" So I stopped her and told her I wanted to buy a computer, and I asked if a salesperson could help me. Her response? "I'm sorry, I can't help you—I'm *just* in customer service."

Needless to say, I didn't buy my computer at that store. And true to the statistics, I told many people this story. If that girl had only realized that she, no matter what her job, was *the* person standing between a good customer experience and a bad one, perhaps she would have acted differently. *Considering yourself as your organization's best ambassador is one of the most important things 100% of employees can do to develop more business for your company!*

Can Someone Help Us, Please?

Here's another story from a slightly different angle. Again, I was in another electronics store, this time searching for a specific software program. My husband and three small children accompanied me, and our search seemed to last an eternity. Finally, we decided to ask for assistance. My husband approached an employee, asked him where we could find the software, and was told that he "didn't know the stock on the floor very well." He referred us to the information desk. As we trudged through congested people-and-merchandise-filled aisles with little ones and a car seat in tow, my husband informed me that the employee's name badge said he was the store's sales manager.

The story above is an example of an employee who was technically in sales within his organization and had an opportunity to develop business for them. But did he? Are your sales people being as helpful as they could be when given the opportunity to help someone—even if that someone is not a prospect?

There is also a distinct difference between customer service and customer satisfaction. Customer service is simply delivering a product or service to the customer that pleases them. Customer satisfaction asks the question: Do they remain satisfied after they've received the product or service? Everyone should have a thorough understanding of what customers expect from him or her so they can give the customer more of what they need to be truly satisfied.

We each have a golden opportunity to *influence* business development. If a customer were to say to you, "I'm not sure. What would you do?" or "What do you think?" What would you say? What do you think your co-workers would say?

In his book, *Selling for Dummies*, Tom Hopkins talks about a customer's itch cycle or period of time before they decide to upgrade to a newer item. Experts have said that the "itch cycle" for purchasing a car, for example, is less than three years. What is your customer's itch cycle? If you don't know, go ask the employees who deal with customers directly. Ask them questions like, what are customers saying they want? How often do they ask for a particular product or service? How would you suggest we help our customers buy additional products that fill a greater need?

Exercising the principle of sincere helpfulness will enable you and your employees to stand out in the crowd. Business development will be influenced in a positive way and your external connections will be stronger and more plentiful. Another added benefit especially in today's competitive market for recruiting good employees: when employees feel appreciated by you and their co-workers, they will have greater job satisfaction. That means when they are faced with an opportunity to stay at your company or move on to another company, they are more likely to stay!

Putting Principle 2 Into Action

Re-design your outbound correspondence to include information bites. For example, each time you send a fax to anyone, you have an opportunity to educate, entertain, inspire, or create awareness of something people may not know about your company. Your fax cover sheet should never be just a fax cover sheet and your e-mail should never be just e-mail. Include some basic information about the company or some simple "Did you know?" facts and other forms of communication. But keep it simple! No one likes clutter, nor will they read it if it is too long. And, keep your messages changing so people actually look forward to getting your stuff.

Encourage employees to send their direct customers "Thought you'd like to know" messages with new product information, news about on the job changes, and other announcements. Handwritten notes can be attached to any corporate documents and are much better at conveying personal messages. If some employees are uncomfortable with writing, help them by giving them a couple of sample notes that you have received and liked.

ACTION Practice saying thank you more frequently, more publicly, and more enthusiastically! Consider your Five Groups of Influence™ and ask yourself, "Who can I thank this week?" Thank customers and prospects for their time--preferably in writing. Remember the last time you received a handwritten thank you card in the mail? Have you ever noticed that people often post a thank you note on a wall in their work area? This is an indication that they are proud of it and their contribution that inspired it. It's also an indication that they probably get thank you notes very rarely. Nothing on your to do list will bring you as much satisfaction when completed as the handwritten thank you note.

ACTION Think about all of the things that you could easily share with others. Do an inventory of your hard and the soft assets. For example, consider the time, money, talent, and knowledge you possess, and then share them whenever you can. Encourage employees to share your philosophy about the benefits of sharing time, talent, and knowledge by pointing out the benefits of sincere helpfulness.

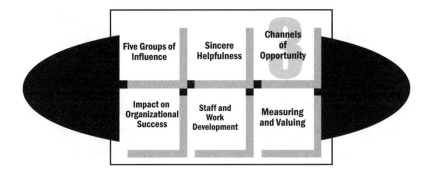

Principle 3

**Knowledge of the primary Channels of Opportunity™
can leverage business development resources.**

It's the question most parents dread because it often comes at a time
when they are least prepared to answer it, "Where do babies come
from?" Our willingness and ability to answer this question begins
to set the stage for how we communicate with our children as they
grow into responsible decision-making adults. On one hand, it's an
easy question to answer, especially since you most likely know the
answer. On the other, depending on the age of the child asking, it
could be difficult to properly describe the origin and overall process
of childbirth.

79

Another question that's more in line with business and poses some difficulty for owners and managers is one that has to do with knowing from where their business comes. Ask yourself: Do you know where your business comes from? Take a couple of minutes right now and list five clients you have had the opportunity to work with recently. Consider listing clients and/or projects you won and some you lost at the proposal stage. Now note how you got the opportunity in the first place. Be specific.

One vice president told us that her company almost never gets business from Request for Proposals (RFP); yet, the single, most lucrative project her office had at that time was a direct result of their response to an RFP listed in an industry trade journal. After our dialogue, the vice president acknowledged that RFPs might be a good channel for them, but couldn't say whether routine perusal of industry trade journals for project leads might be a *viable* channel for business development. Most people say they know how their business was won. After all, it seems obvious once the contract's been awarded, doesn't it? You either get the work from direct sales, repeat business, or referrals. But, let's say that you submit a proposal as a result of a direct sales effort and you get the job. Do you know where the lead originated or how the direct sales effort was initiated in the first place?

Many organizations claim that much of their business comes from word-of-mouth, a noble and effective way to get business. For the purpose of *sharpening* your marketing efforts, though, wouldn't it be useful to know where your referral-based business actually *originates*? Finding out may point to the fact that, for example, a large percentage of your company's business may be influenced by your participation in an annual conference or your monthly involvement in a professional association. In this example, we would call these activities your company's specific Channels of Opportunity™.

In order for employees to be good decision-makers and influencers for a true BDEB culture, and in order for them to leverage their connections and contribute on a business development standpoint, employees must have knowledge and truly understand from where your business comes. Put simply, they must have knowledge of the primary Channels of Opportunity™ for your organization. Throughout this chapter, and with your help, we will demonstrate a process of information gathering that will help you take a closer look at where and how your organization specifically gets both its business and business development opportunities. Through fact finding and reflection, you will begin to identify your organization's most productive Channels of Opportunity™, sorting the prime sirloin from the ground beef, so to speak. By identifying your best Channels of Opportunity™, you can focus a larger portion of your business development resources on the most desirable strategies that reach those channels. You can also decide to focus fewer resources on those activities or approaches that bear little results. You pick the best fruit and leave the rest for the competition.

Do You Know Your Best Channels of Opportunity™?
Roy Gabriel, Vice President of Renaissance Government Solutions (RGS), said after 15 years of sales, he now looks at RGS's business opportunities and his approach to getting new business differently. "I used to think if you bid more jobs, there's a better chance of getting more business," Gabriel said. "Now we take a more focused approach because our win rate is significantly higher when we know about the project before it goes to bid." Knowing their best Channels of Opportunity™ gave RGS a well-informed excuse to re-channel their marketing efforts on the specific activities that bring them business such as building relationships in advance of projects going to bid.

A business consulting firm learned that 90% of their business originated from membership and active participation in their primary professional association. They found that when traced, each business development opportunity went directly to partici-pation in the association by a referral, directory listing, or direct association with a prospect at a chapter meeting. Membership in the association proved to be a gold mine or valuable Channel of Opportunity™ for focused results.

And, in yet another example, one design-build contractor learned that outdoor signage worked wonders for his business. The contractor found that many of his opportunities to quote building projects actually originated from the signage that he placed in front of buildings his company had under construction. Since learning this, he increased his signage and therefore, his business development results. He learned where to formalize and focus his business development efforts.

Quantity vs. Quality

On average, it takes seven meaningful contacts with viable pros-pects to convert them to a customer. You have probably found that this "law of numbers" concept works to increase your business vol-ume as well. Consider the following factors that influence our busi-ness development efforts:

- The number of proposals or quotes your business has submitted
- The number of contacts with potential business prospects employees make
- The number of qualified leads your company has to call on

One often overlooked consideration is the volume and type of work you actually want to do. You may already have the amount of business that you want, but is it the *kind of work* you want to do? When you work to uncover your organization's best Channels of Opportunity™, you can use this new information to be more selective about *who* you do business with.

For example, many companies are [sometimes painfully!] aware of having too much business every time they look at the work on their desks and consider their project deadlines. Law firms are a good example of this judging by the height of their attorneys' case files on desks, credenzas, floors, and guest chairs! (Ever hear of a filing cabinet?) These companies may not want to simply develop more business—instead, *they may want to qualify their prospects for better quality and more prosperous work.* Exploring your organization's Channels of Opportunity™ enables companies to do just that by identifying more profitable and desirable business opportunities— the best fruit on the tree.

Go back to your list of clients and/or projects. Now add the approximate dollar amount and whether you won or lost the project. One purpose of pulling together this information is to document the history of your proposals and add on projects. With all of the information displayed, you will see evidence of interesting trends within your business development activities. You will see patterns in the types of projects on which you are bidding and will be prompted to think of the reasons for losing certain jobs. You also can begin to put a price on your business development opportunities. It's important for both managers and employees to know what their individual projects and clients are worth and what they can afford to spend to attract and retain more of the same.

What's the Price of a Customer For Your Business?
One association executive found their average member contributed $1,535 in annual profit and remained a member for an average of 5.2 years. As a result, they realized that they could afford to spend a little more to attract and retain members.

Analyzing Your Channels of Opportunity™

Look at your business in a way that goes beyond your financial reports. Attorney Alan Rivers calls this "thinking from the 30,000 foot level," like looking down from a plane. The information you've just compiled looks at only five clients and/or projects. We recommend that you expand this work at some point by creating a Channels of Opportunity™ worksheet using data from a one to two-year period. This is important because you don't want to make any major decisions from short-term data.

For example, if your goal is to double the number of projects you do next year, you may need to double the number of solid opportunities you get. To help you find the best way to double your opportunities, look at your data and ask yourself these questions: How many lost proposals did you have before you won a project? Why did you lose each project? Did you lose to a competitor or did the prospect decide not to do the work? What are the reasons for losing the work? What are the primary reasons for winning the work? What would it take to double your business from last year? How many new accounts or new projects would you need? How many accounts and/or projects do you typically have to propose to close that number? Which clients or types of clients represent the greatest opportunities for current and future add on work? Which clients or types of clients represent projects and/or accounts from which you'd like to move away?

A word of caution: Sometimes it may be difficult to obtain all of this data, especially if it is not readily available in one place. Be patient as you collect the data—it's worth your time! You may want to interview different individuals within your organization and go to different sources such as archives, filing cabinets, departments, and even regions. In some cases, you might even have to call your client. The bottom line is that once you have all of the information displayed in your Channels of Opportunity™ business profile, the answers you will find within the data makes the effort well worth your time investment!

According to many experts, the most overlooked business development opportunities are right under your nose. They are:

· The accounts you already sell and serve

- Other divisions, operations and locations of existing customers
- Past customers who stopped buying or for whom you completed a project
- Referrals from clients, suppliers, employees
- Past proposals who didn't buy at the time

Time Well Spent

When asked to review the status of a company's proposals and requests for information, the secretary found that the company hadn't followed up with one municipal inquiry. After tracking it down, they realized that they had inadvertently overlooked this prospect. The company followed up with the municipality, submitted a proposal, and won the business. The resulting contract amount was one of the largest accounts for their company.

The creation of a database or some other type of tool for tracking business development opportunities and information is very important for managing all of your business development opportunities. Without one, companies may lose sales momentum and perspective on opportunities they have within their reach. Many organizations focus too much on getting new leads and not enough on managing the leads they have. The point of BDEB is that with the proper tools and information, everyone in an organization can be responsible for the care and maintenance of those slip-through-the-cracks business development opportunities. While these leads may not be "hot," they are worthy of attention, and who better to help follow up on them but the very people who could possibly be working on the project someday?

In order to get the most informed view of what influences your business development, it is important to further clarify the connections that led to the acquisition of the business. Now you're ready to give credit where credit is due. What we're going to have you do is peel the proverbial onion that represents your business development efforts. Our approach is to look at each layer of connections that have an influence on your ability to get the business. As you peel away each layer, you'll find more good stuff in terms of information that reveals your Channels of Opportunity™.

Next to each client and/or proposal on your list, write your answer to the question, "How did you get this opportunity to quote?" Be specific. Were they a repeat customer? Were they referred from another customer or prospect? Write in their name and a brief description. To help us clarify where our business comes from, we use the following descriptors: Friend Network, Repeat Business, Place of Business, Association and/or Organization Involvement, Direct Advertising & Marketing, Direct Sales Effort, and Referral/Word-of-Mouth. Each descriptor is really a Channel of Opportunity™ and fits into at least one of the Five Groups of Influence™. You will find that they are common to most businesses. Of course, you may have additional descriptors that are unique to your business; however, in order to see distinct patterns in how business comes your way, we urge you to be consistent in your labeling.

Channel of Opportunity™ Descriptors

Friend Network (Group of Influence: Community) - Your Friend Network is your circle of friends and personal contacts in business --people you meet through industry associations, church or social affiliations, business associates and former employees, family, and friends. These are individuals with whom you may or may not routinely share dialog. Many people dislike selling to friends; however, your friend network can be a powerful source of business development opportunities through little or no effort on your part. Your friends simply need know and understand what you do and what your company sells.

Your ultimate goal in communicating to your Friend Network is to continue to share what you can to the very people who are in the best position to refer business to you. It is crucial to maintain top-of-mind awareness with our friends, and they need to hear from you on a consistent ongoing basis.

The Power of Friendships in Business
During our research to validate the BDEB principles in this book, we had the opportunity to visit with Bob Massie, president of Massie & Associates, a marketing consulting firm. During our conversation, he shared the exciting news of his most recent and lucrative contracts—the kind on which businesses are built. Out of curiosity, we asked him how he got the opportunity to bid on one of the contracts, and he replied that the prospect had called him, having been referred to him by a friend.

Later in the conversation, Bob mentioned another contract. We asked him the same series of questions and eventually learned that *each piece of business had come to him either directly or indirectly from friends.* Routinely catching up with his friends seemed like a luxury to this busy entrepreneur, and unfortunately, Bob hadn't planned any communications with the very Channels of Opportunity™ that contributed to much of his business success. Yet early on, Bob had said that he was interested in growing his business. We suggested that he focus on his Friend Network for new business by sending a letter to people within his friend network and thanking them for continuing to think about his company.

Repeat Business (Group of Influence: Clients) - This category represents the clients who call you back for additional projects. It also refers to additions to an existing contract and change orders that add more work resulting in a higher project fee (add-ons).

Place of Business (Group of Influence: Supplier and Community) Sometimes business opportunities present themselves as a result of where your business is physically located. Is your organization located on a floor with other businesses? Perhaps you have offices in a shared office environment? If your organization is located in its own building, your building signage along a busy thoroughfare could promote business opportunities.

Location, Location, Location

Over the years, we have actually acquired a fair amount of business as a result of where our offices were located. One building landlord referred our training services to his colleagues at the collision repair business he previously owned. In another location, the office managers and staff at our shared office facility routinely told our company story to other tenants. While located at that facility, one of the other tenants referred us to his associates in his company's South Carolina headquarters, who in turn hired us for a four-year training contract. Another tenant became a valued subcontractor, bringing us another piece of business that lasted over the course of five years. In every example, we helped our neighbors understand what we did for a living by using our information bite and answering their specific questions. More importantly, we showed an interest in what our neighbors did for a living, and in some cases, we were able to refer business to them. We also shared useful information when appropriate and ultimately became a valuable resource to these people, a fact that continues long after we relocated to different office space.

Association/Organization Involvement (Group of Influence: Community) - This is one category that can be a valuable business development channel for any business. These are the business opportunities that result from your organization's involvement in trade associations, and community organizations. These groups are not to be taken lightly because they can contribute to much of your business growth and success. Unfortunately, many professionals register for a monthly meeting, after having evaluated the meeting topic and/or venue, only to cancel at the last minute due to a hectic schedule. Yet, visibility at routine membership functions is a critical component of participation. You need to be looking at expanding participation, not screening for it. Just remember that you may need to first search for the organizations from which you can most benefit. When you properly value this part of your life, you can make decisions regarding membership and participation differently. What is the dollar value of a missed opportunity when you decide to skip an association meeting? What could you expect in business development opportunities if 50% of your employees participated in some type of industry, trade, or business organization?

Professional Associations Abound

There are many professional associations with the single-minded goal to support its members in the advancement of their craft. Human resource professionals, engineers, facility managers, sales and marketing, and legal assistants all have the opportunity to benefit from membership in organizations designed specifically for them and their professions. When you look at the wealth of learning and networking to learn that goes on at these meetings, it's hard to ignore the value of membership. In their private lives, employees participate in a multitude of activities. It's inappropriate to encourage employees to be in "sales" mode at these activities, but it is entirely acceptable to encourage their commitment to positively and proactively representing themselves and their company to everyone with whom they come in contact.

Direct Advertising & Marketing (Group of Influence: Prospects) - This category represents business development opportunities that result from trade shows, paid advertising (phone book, newspaper, magazine, broadcast, outdoor), direct mail, promotional campaigns/ incentives, phone book & directory listings, signage on company vehicles, newsletters, publicity, authoring an article for publication, telemarketing, special event/open house, and networking. With so many direct advertising strategies available, it is well worth the time spent to further track which method worked best for your organization.

Direct Sales Effort (Group of Influence: Prospects and Employees)
The sales call is one of the most obvious ways to get business and
either begins as a cold call to a target that you've identified as a
business that could use your product or service or as a "warm" call
to a prospect referred to you by another one of your channels. Direct sales efforts include those situations where a sales person initiated the call—no lead provided; the sales person initiated the call—
lead provided; and a prospect called you requesting information.

We define a lead as an unqualified prospect since there is no known
business opportunity. It is a suggestion of an opportunity--a whiff
of new business potential begging to be explored. Leads occur when
someone sees a possible connection between your business and that
of another and suggests you call on them. This happens all the time
in "tip groups" and "lead clubs." Leads can also be found as information you read that inspires follow-up to determine its validity as
sales opportunities for your business. Anything can be a lead, but it
doesn't turn into a qualified prospect until you have discovered that
the prospect needs what you can offer. While all leads are valuable,
some leads have a low payoff. These might include "bingo response
cards," offers for free literature, free sample requests, etc.

Referral/Word-of-Mouth (Group of Influence: Suppliers, Clients,
Employees, and Community) - Referrals are a result of great customer service, networking, or just plain good will. Third party referrals can come from current and past customers, competitors,
friends of the business, employees or contract personnel, and professional contacts. Word-of-mouth, on the other hand, tends to be
an image builder much more than a call to action, says Jerry Wilson. It works in combination with other forms of promotions such

as advertising and should not supplant a formal marketing approach. Wilson says that word-of-mouth can and should be managed for a business to be successful at developing business through this channel.

This category is one of the hardest channels to track unless you are in the habit of asking the callers how they heard about you and your company. You may be in the habit of asking this question, but are your employees? Incoming phone calls usually follow a certain path throughout your organization considering each caller's specific reason for calling. If a call ends with the receptionist, she should ask how they heard about your company. If the call travels to the sales department and someone other than a salesperson takes the call, he should find out how the caller heard about your company.

Now that we've discussed the various connections that influence your business development, it's time for you to go back to your list of five clients and/or proposals and your first layer of connections. Dig deeper to find your second layer of connections by asking how you met the customer in the first place. Let's say you credit a project as repeat customer business. Did they call you as a result of being referred to you? Did they see your advertising? Did you meet them at a trade show? Be specific, using the categories from the Five Groups of Influence™ listed above to help you.

By the time you get to your third layer of connections, it might be getting harder to remember where each connection originated. That's O.K., because that's a sign that you are getting some good insight into your business development efforts.

To find your connection in layer three, determine how you connected in layer two. For example, let's say the customer learned about your organization at a trade show. What originally connected you to the trade show? Did you read about it in a magazine? Did someone you respect recommend that you participate? Is it an industry show that you do annually? Again, be specific. Document which trade show. You may find one or two specific trade shows reoccur as Channels of Opportunity™ for your business.

The data that results from this exercise is often overlooked in the flurry of proposal activity and project work. The problem many people have is remembering the details of each proposal. By going through a step-by-step process of recording the generations of business opportunity, you will be asking this question to help you remember these valuable clues to your organization's business development success. We have even allowed for a fourth generation of connections if necessary. Here is an actual example of one of our projects that went as far as four generations.

Layer 1	Layer 2	Layer 3	Layer 4
Direct Sales: Sales rep sold to client after months of relationship building, proposal, and follow-up.	Direct Advertising and Marketing: Met company at a technical trade show in November at the convention center.	Association Involvement: Asked by executive director of our industry association to speak at a breakout session; were given exhibit space at show.	Association Involvement: Maintain annual membership in industry association and regularly attend monthly meetings.

Now it's time to evaluate where your business truly originates. Peeling back the layers of connections can help you formally justify where you should put more energy, time, and monetary resources. Before you study your data, consider that we have purposely not created a lot of structure within the evaluation portion of this exercise because every business and situation is unique. You need room to make your own assessments and conclusions from this activity.

Look for the reoccurrence of certain Channels of Opportunity™ and specific patterns in your data. How often do you see repeat business or referrals from industry peers? Since it takes three or more data points to indicate a trend, we suggest you look at your data and begin to plot what you see. Your worksheet could look something like this:

Example	Channels of Opportunity™			
	Layer 1	Layer 2	Layer 3	Layer 4
1	Referral	Place of business	Direct advertising	Friend Network
2	Trade Show	Industry Association	Friend Network	
3	Add-on project (Repeat)	Referral	Direct sales	Place of business
4	Add-on project (Repeat)	Industry Association	Friend Network	
5	Repeat business	Direct sales	Trade Show	Industry Association

If you were to plot the results from your data, you would begin to see business development strategies emerge that are strong ones for your specific organization, your products and services, and your overall employee connections. Simply count how many times you see each Channel of Opportunity™. In the example above, four channels emerge as strengths because they appear more than other channels: Direct advertising (trade shows being the dominant), Industry Association, Repeat Business, and Friend Network.

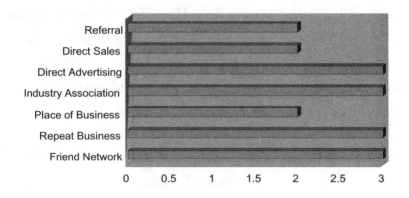

In many instances, there is no ultimate root cause or single origination point for your business development opportunities. For example, your advertising supports the sale by getting the message out about your products and services and creates additional awareness, especially if prospects have also heard about your company through their friends, the community, and your sales staff.

Your goal in considering your Channels of Opportunity™ should be to think through the primary connections that have influenced your ability to quote work. When you have finished with this exercise, you will have a composite sketch highlighting how a variety of connections have influenced business opportunities and a clearer picture that shows from where your business comes. These connections can then be categorized as your primary Channels of Opportunity™ and shared as useful information with employees for leveraging business development resources. And, don't just share this information with your employees; help them see the value of their connections by pointing out that they do influence new business in their daily work. Next, we'll discuss your organization's attitudinal fitness for valuing connections and the activities that contribute to a productive BDEB environment.

Are You Attitudinally Fit for BDEB?

There are really only three ways to get more business:

1. Increase the number of customers you sell to and serve
2. Increase the average sales to current customers
3. Get your current customers to buy more frequently

For many companies, the single best source of business is increased sales from existing customers. It is the 80/20 Rule at its best—often a full 80% of our business comes from 20% of our clients. Diana Callahan, owner of Cake Create, a commercial distribution center and chain of retail stores in the bakery supply industry, has boiled this concept down for her employees. In an effort to retain the 20% of customers that create 80% of her sales, Callahan gives her employees the freedom to save the relationship by telling them, "Don't lose a customer over something you can solve for a little bit of money." Over the years, she has learned that you can correct almost any customer issue for as little as $25, a nominal amount if the customer remains satisfied and continues to shop there and refer business to the store.

Do your employees know how your company wins its business? Are you *sure* they know? We've observed that most managers believe employees know how sales are made, while in fact, employees are uninformed and therefore, ill-equipped for BDEB. When employees know the facts supporting your company's specific Channels of Opportunity™, they can contribute to business development by seeking additional ways to provide client service. That is why you must create this awareness and encourage the types of activities that win additional client business. Callahan and her husband are very community-focused, devoting a lot of their time to community service endeavors. As a result, Callahan says that much of Cake Create's business is due to word-of-mouth marketing, and she credits her employees for providing good service that keeps customers coming back and recommending their products to others.

When 100% of employees are doing these types of activities, your business will increase exponentially. You'll have prospects calling *you*, having heard great things about your company. Track these calls and the individual impact of community involvement, advertising, and other forms of marketing. You can do this during team meetings, on an activity database through your company Intranet, or with weekly management reports.

Many effective business development activities are ones that seem spontaneous and mundane. They are the chance meetings that occur when you take the time to attend a networking event or visit with your neighbor. They are the casual conversations you have with strangers in a coffee shop. What are some not-so-obvious BDEB activities that can result in business development opportunities for your organization? Going from chance or haphazard, to planned and intentional can make activities possibly considered overhead on a marketing budget a profitable payoff. One key to success from performing these activities is your *business development attitude*. We have often said that you can train employees on the skills and knowledge needed to do their jobs well, but it is very hard to teach the proper attitudes it takes for ultimate job success.

For example, think back to your last pleasant fast food experience. O.K., if that's a hard one, think about your last *unpleasant* fast food experience. See how quickly that memory comes to mind? One of the biggest problems the fast food industry faces (and any industry that pays minimum wage) is hiring people who possess the right kind of attitudes to provide quality customer service. Every now and then you'll find the one shining example of the model employee—the person, and age doesn't matter here—who looks you in the eye, smiles, and asks you how they can help you. Or, they look you in the eye, smile, and thank you for your business! Author Jerry Wilson calls these the "we care" people. Whatever the situation, attitude is the foundation for creating a BDEB culture.

Life is full of the mundane. Everyday we find ourselves doing things that we might grumble about such as waiting in lines and in crowded lobbies, riding elevators, and traveling on public transportation. We have a choice, as do our employees, how we perceive these activities. We can choose to be inquisitive and positive about life, using this time productively to positively and proactively represent our organization. Or, we can choose to be negative, completing these tasks with eyes down and lips locked.

Being "attitudinally fit" for BDEB means that you acknowledge all of life's interactions as possible opportunities for business development. You are looking through the proverbial rose-colored glasses at activities that you might otherwise consider "time munchers." But, what if you could demonstrate that 30% of your business opportunities actually come from doing activities such as attending after-hours networking events, routinely visiting a coffee shop and getting to know its patrons, or even attending your spouse's office party? Would they still seem mundane? From a business development standpoint, knowing what your best (and often underestimated) Channels of Opportunity™ are is one of the best ways to make decisions about how you should spend your time and where you devote your sales and marketing efforts. Put simply, those "time munchers" might actually be the best thing for your organization. Fully understanding these facts can actually change your mind about the activities.

Of course, this does not replace a solid sales process. It simply <u>feeds</u> the sales process. Using food as the metaphor, let's say that you've got the stew prepared and on the stove. All you've got to do to get it ready to eat is turn up the temperature. Finding your company's Channels of Opportunity™ is about helping you turn up the temperature in your business development efforts. There is no need to start over with your sales and marketing efforts, and there is certainly no need to do an in-depth analysis about who you are and what you do. Once you uncover where your business actually comes from and what activities net more business, you must simply turn up the temperature on those activities for more sales!

Putting Principle 3 Into Action

Consider assembling a cross-functional project team of two to four people to complete the Channels of Opportunity™ exercise. By handpicking some people who have a lot to gain from understanding from where your business "really" comes, you can actually accomplish many things while gathering some great organizational data.

· Have everyone on the project team read the Channels of Opportunity™ chapter in this book.

· As a group, decide how to best divide the work at hand. Different individuals may have better access, and therefore, an easier time finding certain data.

· Set deadlines for data gathering and schedule the next meeting.

Ready, Aim, Fire

Regarding spending too much time on the Channels of Opportunity™ exercise: Members of the National Speakers Association use the "ready, fire, aim" theory in their marketing development. It reminds us that at some point you have to say "enough already" and get on with your planning. If you wait to get the perfect shot (ready, aim, fire) you will get caught up in the "paralysis of analysis." You'll never get 100% of the data together—so move on when trends emerge that can be acted on immediately.

ACTION Have a Channels of Opportunity™ work group present their findings to the rest of the employees. Write a summary of findings and distribute to everyone. Get everyone involved in developing ideas to maximize your unique Channels of Opportunity™.

ACTION With input from the Channels of Opportunity™ exercise, have your management team examine the findings with this question in mind: What specific types of projects and/or clients does your company want more of? Base your decisions on desired criteria such as (but not limited to) profit potential, market trends, and satisfaction level. You might find that your largest or highest dollar volume accounts aren't always the most valuable or profitable. You must look at the costs to serve the account, the demands the client makes, the hassles incurred, etc. One retailer found they were losing money on their largest account due to delivery costs and double-the-average warranty costs.

ACTION To promote add-on or repeat client business, ask all employees to take detailed notes during project and client meetings. Employees should get in the habit of writing down things they hear in these meetings that may not be directly relevant to the project, but could represent future business development opportunities. Encourage them to revisit the notes after the meeting is over and give any leads to senior management. It is important to remind them to not attempt to filter out any notes deemed as irrelevant. If we're doing our job by educating employees on what's important in terms of business development, they will eventually be able to decide whether the information is relevant for business development.

ACTION Master the concept of attitudinal fitness by being attitudinally fit BDEB models. Accept the mundane as opportunities for business development and take advantage of situations that could result in a productive BDEB conversation. Furthermore, start considering the concept of "attitudinal fitness" when hiring new employees.

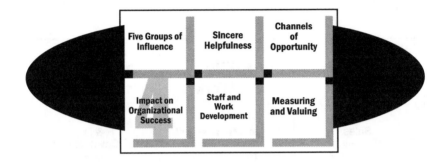

Principle 4

Employees do their best work when they understand how they impact organizational success.

In order for business development to be everyone's business in your organization, employees should understand that what they do impacts the company's business. Sales and marketing people have the advantage in this area because they are more likely to see a direct return on their work activities in terms of sales. Plus, they are probably being evaluated routinely by their sales results! They know what it takes to influence people to buy, and they have an overall understanding of what types of activities it takes to make an impact to the bottom line. Most employees outside the scope of sales are insulated from this knowledge.

Think about how each employee category in your organization contributes to organizational success. Go back to your math in the first principle. How many employees in your organization "Get the Work?" How many "Do the work?" How many "Support the Work?"

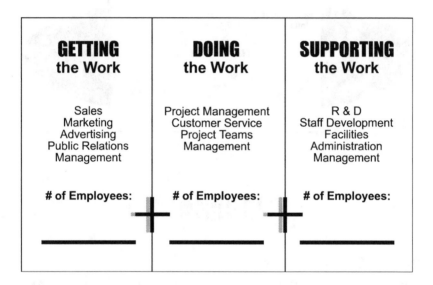

GETTING the Work	DOING the Work	SUPPORTING the Work
Sales Marketing Advertising Public Relations Management	Project Management Customer Service Project Teams Management	R & D Staff Development Facilities Administration Management
# of Employees:	# of Employees:	# of Employees:

Would you get repeat business if project engineers didn't produce within the project scope? Would your cash flow be as solid if invoices weren't processed in a timely manner? How happy would your customers be if their order wasn't delivered when it was ready? (For example, in the food industry, unless you order a cold sandwich, receiving a cold sandwich is not a good thing.)

As companies have discovered, there are many sound business reasons to help employees understand their impact on your organization. Here are a few of them.

106

Understanding Personal Impact Increases Confidence

When your confidence goes up, your competence goes up at the same time. Like the flea said to the elephant after they, together, had crossed the bridge, "Boy, did we shake that thing, or what?!" Even as small as the flea was, he believed that he impacted the bridge as they walked over. It is a fact: When employees recognize their individual impact on customer satisfaction, the sales cycle, and creating greater public awareness, they gain greater confidence to do more for the company.

Confidence breeds success, which furthers the attitudes and behaviors that support a BDEB environment. If you don't believe this, think about how you felt on your first day on the job. Remember feeling insecure, and yes, even a little worthless, because you didn't know one-tenth of what you know now? Remember what it felt like to take that first phone call from a customer? It's a proven fact that employees' attitudes will change as they learn about the company and how to do their jobs better. And, more information and knowledge gives employees the ability to look for ways the company can improve product and service quality.

Consider the alternatives to confidence: insecurity, instability, and uncertainty. Would you want employees with these attributes working for you? Would your customers want to work with these employees? In today's competitive job market, employees who know how and what they contribute to the bottom line are more likely to stay with an organization. (And, with their knowledge and expertise, you are more likely to WANT them to stay with your organization!) Employees should have clear-cut direction on what they should be doing, and they should know how to do extra things to enhance their relationships with fellow employees, suppliers, and customers.

Employee's Small Contribution to Company's BIG Goal
One large insurance company told their employees that in spite of beating the current year's production goals, they had to produce an additional $20 million in revenue before year-end. This was a significant increase to be accomplished in a very short time frame. Department heads told all their direct reports the new organizational goals and reminded them that they supported the sales force in very important ways. Together they brainstormed ways they could provide the needed support to the sales force.

When later asked how her job impacted the company's ability to reach this goal, one employee in the training department said she contributed by resolving internal staff and organizational problems that may delay underwriting of policies or closing of deals. This confident approach to doing her job has had high payoff for the company in terms of this employee's high performance and company loyalty.

When employees are properly informed, they are more likely to assume the degree of personal responsibility necessary for the success of the organization. Employees fundamentally know that they need to maintain a solid foundation of knowledge about the company and its clients so that when there is a special need in the business, such as producing an extra $20 million in revenue, it won't be such a stretch to achieve new goals. This type of information frequently changes though, and in many cases, employees need ongoing management support to maintain this knowledge.

"Knowledge is Power"
At USA Group, an Indianapolis-based administrator and guarantor of education loans, middle and senior management participate in bi-monthly "leadership forums" to discuss financial data, updates on marketing, newest gains and losses, and a projection of how well the company is progressing toward fiscal year end bonuses. Managers, in turn, are encouraged to pass this information along to their employees in routine staff meetings, stressing the importance of the "knowledge is power" concept.

Employees have access to a lot of information when they first join a company. They receive employee handbooks, operation manuals, and other tools that help them quickly get acclimated to the culture of the organization and their individual job roles. Some organizations put new employees through rigorous training, introducing them to everything they will need to know in order to do their jobs effectively. ADS Environmental Services, a sewer flow monitoring company based in Huntsville, Alabama, puts all new employees regardless of position through what they call "Sewer University™." Employees participate in a week long school where they learn the history and philosophy of the company, how ADS equipment operates, and differences between their equipment and that of competitors.

Michael Hammer, author of *Reengineering the Corporation* says, "The single-most important thing you can do to help your company thrive is: Help every single person in the company understand the business in the same 'big picture' terms that the CEO does. Everyone needs to understand the economics of the company and its industry, its strategy and cost structure, its processes, products, and competitors." He points out that this knowledge can lead to changed behaviors that are – "customer-focused, team-oriented, results-seeking, and self-starting." Here is a good example of a client and supplier relationship that demonstrates a mutually strong foundation of knowledge about each other's business.

Letting the People "In the Know" Handle the Problem

A packaging team at Campbell's was having problems with boxes breaking. After talking with the packaging crew about the problem, Campbell's managers realized that members of the packaging crew were probably the ones who should talk directly with the supplier. When the managers called the supplier to tell them they would be hearing from their packaging crew regarding the problem, their supplier suggested that the crew talk directly to *their* hourly employees who were best suited to solve the problem!

Campbell's managers believe that if they had tried to solve this problem without the individuals who were directly involved, the problem would have gone on forever. Their solution was to rent a van and send their people to their supplier's place of business. Together, they solved the whole thing. "It gave the workers great confidence," said Ron Ferner, Former V.P. of Low-Cost Business Systems at Campbell's Soup Co. "That never would have happened in the days when Campbell's had a policy of not telling anybody anything that wasn't written down for them."

This example shows how the people who are impacted by a customer problem are the very people to solve it in an organization. Empowering employees to get the job done is one of the best ways to increase job satisfaction because employees feel valued, trusted, and included as an important part of the client relationship. Sharing customer feedback with employees is also a powerful motiva-tor—both positive and negative feedback! Here is another example:

Seeing Impact is Believing Impact

One company had a large rush job from one of its largest customers. The owner explained the situation to his production people and together they determined how to get the job done within the timeframe requested by the customer. The customer, in turn, was pleased and expressed his appreciation to the owner. But the owner didn't stop there—he wisely took this praise a step further by asking his client if his production people could visit his facility and see first hand how their efforts impacted the customer's business. The customer hosted a tour and the production people got to see first hand how their work fit into the customer's larger production job or the "big picture" of the overall project. The production people came back feeling appreciated—reinforcing their efforts to get the job done. It was a win-win situation for everyone.

Often, the "big picture" of your business and your customer's busi-ness is lost on employees. Mission statements try hard to succinctly illustrate the big picture of an organization, but often fail because they are considered clichéd and unbelievable by employees. The example above illustrates one of the best ways to help employees buy in to your organization's mission statement—getting them in-volved and letting them see through their own eyes the result of your organization's products and services on your client organiza-tions.

Why not provide training focused on key business principles that illustrate how employees can improve profitability and customer satisfaction within their existing departments? Basic business aware-ness is a hot training topic among businesses that are interested in leveraging their employee resources. The reason is due in part to the fact that businesses are seeking new ways in which to motivate and inspire employees to be productive contributors to the bottom line. And, how do employees know how to do this if they have limited understanding and knowledge of the company's financials?

Employee Impact on the Bottom Line

Jack Sweeney has found that most employees value the opportunity to understand the decision-making process and to learn how their individual actions affect the entire company's performance. The company recently initiated a quarterly profit sharing program based on the company's performance. Sweeney's goal was to provide training to all employees in order to enable them to fully understand their impact on the bottom line and to see firsthand how they could personally benefit by making greater contributions. To promote this knowledge, Sweeney held a daylong financial workshop for his entire company, which consisted of mostly shop floor employees. During the workshop, he taught them how to read Langsenkamp's income statements and balance sheets to see how the company generated its profits.

A software development and implementation company was struggling with the amount of rework that needed to be done on a number of their implementation projects. The rework delayed payment of the company's invoices, which forced the company to borrow money to pay operating expenses—particularly salaries. Borrowing costs in the form of interest caused the profit of the company to suffer, and line of credit availability was negatively impacted making cash flow a problem for the company. The problem was that most of the company's employees did not understand the concept of cash flow and its impact on the business.

Forty employees participated in company-specific business awareness training, called Enterprise Profitability, which included three separate sessions and an in-depth explanation of the company's income statement and balance sheet. After employees took the course, the president of the company observed that they began doing a better job of "doing it right the first time." Billings were being paid because the work was acceptable, cash flow improved, and the company was able to pay off its line of credit for the first time in three years.

Understanding personal impact encourages employee retention.

Assuming more personal responsibility gives employees a chance to shine. Confidence boosts greater self-esteem, better morale, greater company loyalty and higher business development performance. And, don't forget about employee retention. Studies show that happy employees are loyal employees. In a job market glutted with 4% unemployment, an abundance of available jobs, and not enough qualified workers, economic and environmental incentives play a huge role in employees' willingness to select and stay with your organization.

Based on a survey and an analysis by the Gallup Organization, the most critical factors bearing on employees' satisfaction and job performance seem to be the following:

· Employees have the opportunity every day to do what they do best.

· A supervisor or someone at work seems to care about them as people.

· At work, employees' opinions seem to count.

· Over the past year, employees have had opportunities to learn and grow.

· The mission of their employer makes employees feel that their jobs are important.

· Employees have the materials and equipment to do their work right.

· Employees' companies are "family friendly."

How your employees feel about their work is reflected in their work performance. What are your employees saying about working for you?

"I feel good about what I do, and I get recognized for good work. If someone tells my boss that I did a nice job on something, I'll get a real congratulations from him."

"I feel as if my opinions count a lot, and I've been instrumental in making changes. My boss isn't hands-off, but loves what I do and tells me to run with it. It's neat to have that much freedom."

"When I first came here and the CEO not only gave us the financials but expected us to learn them, I was astounded. We felt respected. And now we use those numbers to improve."

Understanding personal impact facilitates exceptional customer satisfaction.

Not only do you win more business, but you can also keep customers longer. You can spend all the money in the world in product development, but if your employees somehow alienate potential buyers, or fail to meet their needs, the business doesn't stand a chance against its competitors. Who in your organization gets formally "trained" on company policy, marketing practices, and product information? Is it the employees who are naturally on the front line with customers such as your receptionist, administrative assistants, call center employees, member services personnel, the lunchroom cashier, and accounts receivable employees? Or, is it just your outside sales force?

These are not the only employees influencing customer satisfaction. Those persons behind the scenes in departments such as administration, product development, human resources, training, and property management, to name a few, have tremendous influence. By being recognized and rewarded for the role they play in business development for the organization, employees naturally increase their contributions to business development . . .and their value to the bottom line. Here is a good example of how employees can leverage their networks and sphere of influence to actually find opportunities for more business.

Innovation and Opportunity Equals Earning

Roy Davis has worked for Langsenkamp for 37 years as a fabricator. In addition to working for Langsenkamp, Roy has also worked part time for almost the same length of time for a Budweiser distributor. At his part time job, he performs routine maintenance on delivery trucks.

Recently, Roy recognized an opportunity to connect the two businesses. He saw that the distributor's truck drivers needed ramps to get carts from the street to the sidewalk, so he asked permission to build a sample dock board for them to try. Roy used scrap material to build a sample dock board that provided a smoother transition from the street to the sidewalk, and delivered it with a quote. The distributor said that the dock board was the best thing they had ever seen, and they placed an order with Langsenkamp for the first time.

Understanding personal impact enables a better ability to promote within the ranks.

The book *301 Great Management Ideas* has a great management idea about engaging workers in entry-level jobs. The book tells the story of Zingerman's Delicatessen in Ann Arbor, Michigan. Of the 52 upper level managers, 44 came from within the employee ranks over the years. This was made possible because of Zingerman's commitment to providing employees with lots of information, listening to ideas and suggestions, and giving staff a financial stake in the company.

Zingerman's Deli

The primary job of the co-owner of Zingerman's is to sell the company's principles to the staff of 140 people. Week after week, he reiterates how important employees' jobs are. Employees receive a hefty monthly newsletter detailing new products, departmental news, and the company's direction. The newsletter also reviews business books. The restaurant chain posts weekly sales and labor costs, and has open monthly meetings where management reviews profit-and-loss statements. All employees are eligible for profit sharing after one year of employment. The co-owner says that this practice requires more training, but the payoff is worth it. The employees already understand the company and its customers, which is the most difficult thing to teach new hires.

Understanding personal impact promotes better negotiation skills.

Work environments have evolved into more empowerment cultures where decision-making is being pushed down to managers, supervisors, and team members. As a result, good negotiations skills have become important as people manage their jobs, direct reports, and departments. Good negotiators know their company's position on certain matters, and they have the authority to say yes or no. In order for employees to effectively negotiate, they too need to feel comfortable with their basic knowledge of their company, its financial situation, and processes. Basic business knowledge reinforces any negotiation skills they acquire through training.

"Driving" Authority Down

Saturn was one of the first car manufacturers to drive authority down to the person making the sale. The company's "no hassle, no haggle" sales policy keeps customers coming back because they don't feel bullied, manipulated or pressured to buy. Saturn specifically recruits employees who are enthusiastic participants in the company's overall philosophy and have strong communication and problem solving skills. Along with being given the authority to complete the sales transaction, Saturn employees are well trained in the company's mission, vision, and values, product knowledge and availability.

Saturn highlights its BDEB-familiar philosophy in one of its television commercials. As the car salesman explains Saturn's approach to customer service, he adds, "I treat people like I want to be treated. Besides, I might run into one of my customers at the grocery store sometime!"

Understanding personal impact enhances the natural connections for business development opportunities.

Recognizing the personal and professional networks they bring to the table is probably the most often overlooked opportunity for employees to have a positive impact on organizational success. Armed with knowledge from your Channels of Opportunity™,

117

employees can become "walking billboards" for your company. When employees are aware of the activities that it takes to develop business opportunities, they can positively and proactively represent their company to everyone.

Positive Representation Among the "Brush"

An engineering consulting firm in Portland, Oregon encourages its employees to always be on the lookout for new customers. Many of the surveyors at David Evans & Associates are armed with business cards to give to people interested in their services. "You can be out on the job in some pretty rugged areas, and a lot of times someone will come up to you and ask what you are doing there," says Dan Rothermel, a survey technician with the company. That's why Rothermel makes sure he is knowledgeable about the project as well as the company so he is ready for the inevitable questions.

Rothermel believes that employees who do field work have excellent opportunities for business development impact. When they're out on a job site, talking to a contractor, employees have been asked if the company can provide specific services. Those who know have actually helped develop business for the company. Rothermel also believes that the way employees conduct themselves definitely reflects on the company.

Putting Principle 4 Into Action

ACTION Provide all employees with company-specific business awareness training. Formal training is recommended here since employees often recognize it as important and necessary. During these learning sessions, employees should be given information about the company's products and services; mission, vision, values, and financial picture; clients and competitors; and how the company markets its products and services. At USA Group, the Senior Vice President (SVP) of Finance and Senior Vice President of Marketing usually give these overviews to employees. In the company's New Employee Orientation, trainers provide it with the SVPs present to follow up on specific questions.

ACTION Encourage employees, especially project managers and customer service representatives, to set aside reasonable time each week to read business and industry journals and surf the web for relevant information to support their jobs. For example, a department within USA Group provides summaries of industry journals online so people can quickly read them and keep abreast of industry news and information. And, don't stop there! Encourage them to store information and references in client and prospect files as they relate. Catch your employees reading up and say thank you!

ACTION Encourage employees to summarize what they learn through their reading and to share it with other employees. Perhaps specialty areas based on expertise and interest could be created so certain employees can limit their reading. Some bookstores require store employees to become expert at certain sections, encouraging them to read many of the books in their section. This strategy enables store employees to provide a higher level of customer service.

ACTION Have a tabletop or wall display in plain view for every department of your company. (We mentioned this idea briefly in the first chapter.) The display could show who that department's customers are, the products or services it provides, and the resources available to other employees. For example, if your company is a supplier to Red Gold, remind employees how what they do affects Red Gold products by displaying various product cans. Individual employees could be responsible periodically for supplying something to the display such as a relevant article, job aid, or professional development idea. The purpose of the display is to keep all employees informed about your organization and your client organizations.

ACTION Encourage employees to write an article about a topic of their expertise or passion. The dictionary defines the word "passion" as a strong liking for or devotion to some activity, object, or concept. Passion in the workplace means that the environment is alive with possibility and opportunity. Employees work together productively, creating ideas and completing projects with the company's goals in mind. Passion is contagious. Passion gives you the courage of your convictions.

 **ACTION** When employees, especially leaders, are passionate about something, and they are encouraged to share their passion, others will take note and be inspired to join them. That's why it's so important to encourage the exercise of writing to get thoughts, perceptions, ideas, interpretations, and inspirations out for debate or discussion. The goal is to increase their learning by promoting study, reflection, and idea generation. Articles could then be included in corporate communications, giving all employees the opportunity for recognition.

 **ACTION** Consider implementing a "Who Do You Work For and What Do You Do?" campaign to create an overall awareness of BDEB. (We recommend that you take a humorous communications approach.) Of course, you would expect employees in the direct position of developing business for the company to know the answer to these questions. The goal is to get all employees to the place where they can confidently and comfortably answer these questions and use their information bite, tapping into their knowledge about the company. Part of the campaign could be the use of crossword puzzles, trivia contests, and other games. Consider distributing business cards as a reward for the completion of a "Get to Know the Company" session.

 **ACTION** Walk through your company and randomly ask employees what they understand about your company's critical business issues. Tom Peters calls the process of routinely walking through your company "managing by walking around" (MBWA.) Hollywood calls it "seeing and being seen." Whatever *you* call it, the goal is to remain at the pulse of the work, talking to employees and helping them whenever you can. Show employees that you're receptive to their questions and ideas, and always be on the lookout for opportunities to catch employees doing something right. As you walk around, you might find some employees who need to learn more about your business. Encourage and support them, and try not to put them on the spot. Employees will be ready to meet the challenge if they truly know your company's goals, products, and services.

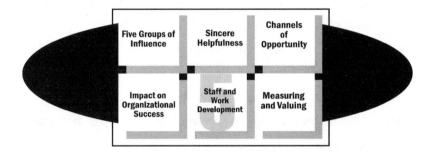

Principle 5

Ongoing staff and work environment development increases organizational potential.

Principle 5 is a critical one because it supports the capacity of your organization and its people to grow and change with the times. In business, every situation is unique and requires flexibility from the organization to be able to meet these situational demands. Contrary to a popular phrase, businesses don't run by themselves. In addition to strong leadership, it takes people—employees—to make things happen and meet the unique challenges presented by all of our connections—clients, suppliers, employees, prospects, and even community.

Ongoing development also supports your organization's capacity or potential to get more of whatever it is that you want--more profits, more satisfied customers, or more productive employees. Few business people will argue against the benefits of ongoing staff and work environment development. Yet, it is an area where many businesses "undersupport." It is a proven fact: Companies that provide routine opportunities for the development of their staff benefit from these investments far more than companies who only occasionally provide development. A study done by the American Management Association found that companies responding to the survey experienced a 68% increase in profits as a result of increasing their training budget during a corporate transition.

In the book, *Competitive Advantage Through People*, Jeffrey Pfeffer recommends that owners and managers consider their staff worthy of constant and diligent development.

> *"Achieving competitive success through people involves fundamentally altering how we think about the work force and the employment relationship. It means achieving success by working with people, not by replacing them or limiting the scope of their activities. It entails seeing the work forces as a source of strategic advantage, not just as a cost to be minimized or avoided."*

If you want your employees to embrace BDEB principles and perform basic BDEB activities, then you need to look at this principle very systematically. To nurture a BDEB culture or philosophy especially if it's a different way of doing things within your organization, you must first establish among your employees the value of a BDEB culture. What's in it for them? Think about what you may already be doing to encourage desired behavior. Performance bonuses? Public recognition? Gift certificates and other incentives? With BDEB, knowledge that employees influence a sale can be a motivator as well. If your organization already has BDEB-like practices in place, you may be reading this book and thinking, "so far, so good." Hopefully, the principles simply confirm your beliefs for the continuation of your excellent employee and management strategies.

We define staff development as anything that is supported by the organization that helps employees do their jobs better. Development could be facilitated in many forms including: technical and/or soft skill training; regularly scheduled staff meetings where everyone has an opportunity to gain and share critical knowledge; inhouse lunch and learns; company-sponsored seminars and workshops; access to and encouraged use of a corporate library; mentoring programs; special assignments; discussion groups, either online or inperson; and hands-on management supervision and feedback, to name a few. We define work environment development as the enhancement of processes, systems, physical space, and/or resources in the environment that influence performance. Many times managers can facilitate improvements in the work environment by simply removing obstacles for employees.

Specific reasons why owners and managers might provide staff development opportunities and improve the current work environment are:

125

- Their goal is to facilitate better working relationships among individual employees and/or whole departments.
- They hope to identify areas for personal and business improvement.
- They want to clarify job roles and performance expectations.
- They want to help employees attain important skills such as goal setting, time management, and conflict resolution.
- They want to foster a BDEB environment in which 100% of employees are involved and contribute to the company's business development efforts.

BDEB Skills Assessment

The BDEB Skills Assessment should help you get started. In an effort to foster BDEB behaviors, it is important to first determine which areas of staff and work environment development you should focus on. We use this assessment tool in our BDEB employee workshop to help individuals determine the areas with the most opportunities to improve. The 30 statements on the next few pages represent behaviors that anyone can do and that you can expect from all employees regardless of their formal role in the organization.

Take a couple of minutes to do this self-assessment. It will help you personally discover where your strengths and weaknesses are concerning business development. It's actually an enlightening activity to do even if your primary responsibility is sales and marketing because some of the statements highlight areas in which we all can improve. We have also included a blank assessment in the Appendix to copy and use for your employees.

The 30 statements on the BDEB Skills Assessment focus on several practical business development ideas that can be immediately implemented in your organization. We recommend that you focus on those activities that you do only "some of the time" or "none of the time" and develop strategies to improve in these areas.

You'll notice that we classified BDEB skills and behaviors into three primary categories: 1) Presenting Yourself; 2) Understanding Your Organization; and 3) Proactive Business Development. Did you score a 40 in all three categories?

BDEB Skills Assessment

Instructions: The following self-assessment relates to how you contribute to business development in your organization. Please write the number that most applies to you next to the statements below. If you write in 3, for example, you believe that you do that activity most of the time. Add up your scores and transfer them to the Assessing My Score section.

4 - All of the time   **3 - Most of the time**   **2 - Some of the time**   **1 - None of the time**

1.   ____I say thank you.

2.   ____I have gotten to know the organization inside and out.

3.   ____I keep my work space clean and neat.

4.   ____I dress professionally and appropriately in the event a client visits our office.

5.   ____I ask questions.

6.   ____I ask for business cards and hand them out often.

7.   ____I am not afraid to say, "I don't know, but I can get that information for you."

8.   ____I obtain company literature showcasing products and services.

9.   ____I know who my company's clients are and what they do.

10.   ____I smile a lot, face to face and over the phone.

11.   ____I ask to be included in decisions, optional projects, and new product launches.

12.   ____I set aside time for making contacts that focus on customer satisfaction.

13.   ____I share my ideas with others.

14.   ____I am aware of who is making decisions, and get to know what they think.

15.   ____I participate in groups in my company to brainstorm best business development practices.

16.   ____I say "I'm sorry" when needed.

17.   ____If I state a problem, I present a possible solution.

18.   ____I am a mentor/coach.

4 - All of the time   **3 - Most of the time**   **2 - Some of the time**   **1 - None of the time**

19.   _____I believe in taking personal responsibility for my actions.

20.   _____I have a complete list of all employees within my company and their phone numbers.

21.   _____I participate in volunteerism in the community.

22.   _____ I document my successes so that I may support my professional advancement.

23.   _____I ask for frequent and timely feedback.

24.   _____I treat my co-workers like they are my customers.

25.   _____When planning my daily to do items, I plan time for interruptions.

26.   _____I try to follow up when I have brought in a business lead.

27.   _____I seek out opportunities to share what I do with others.

28.   _____I return all phone calls promptly.

29.   _____ I try to get the information to do my job well.

30.   _____I send thank you cards and articles to contacts when appropriate.

Assessing Your Score

	Presenting Yourself	Understanding Your Organization	Proactive Business Development
	1. _____	2. _____	3. _____
	4. _____	5. _____	6. _____
	7. _____	8. _____	9. _____
	10._____	11._____	12._____
	13._____	14._____	15._____
	16._____	17._____	18._____
	19._____	20._____	21._____
	22._____	23._____	24._____
	25._____	26._____	27._____
	28._____	29._____	30._____
Totals	_____	_____	_____

40 - 32   Great   You are contributing to business development!

31 - 22   Good   You are doing most of the things it takes to be a contributor in the business development effort.

21 - Below   Needs Improvement   Look for ways to get help in this area. You can start with the ideas on this list.

Presenting Yourself

How you present yourself both in manner and dress speaks volumes about you and your organization. For example, police officers know this and use voice command, presence, and good grooming to diffuse situations that show signs of escalating into violence. Think back to a time when you have been greeted by a person whose appearance was sloppy and their manner unprofessional. What impressions did you walk away with? What impressions do your customers and professional peers have about you and your employees?

Image is Everything

Presenting yourself professionally through good grooming doesn't mean that you have to wear $800 suits. But a little bit of professionalism in your manner of dress does help present the desired image. A friend walked into a furniture store one day and saw two store employees hunched over plates of steaming food, wearing torn t-shirts and dirty jeans . . . and, eating on the merchandise (a table that clearly had a price tag on it.) Thinking this was the warehouse crew, she asked for assistance only to learn these men were the sales staff. Another friend visited a corporate client on what was apparently "casual day." The receptionist was wearing jeans and an untucked flannel shirt; her tennis shoes were dirty and worn. In both these examples, each employee was in the position to greet potential buyers of their company's products. In some companies, this manner of dress might indicate creativity and innovation. But in these two companies, their choice of attire might hint at a lack of respect for customers, themselves, and their companies.

Understanding Your Organization

Have we said enough about the benefits of employees knowing both your business and your clients' businesses? Truly understanding what your organization is about is an important ingredient for employees in their ability to seek and find business development opportunities. Again, think of your employees as "walking billboards" for your company, representing themselves and your organization in all walks of life. The only way they can do this well is by constantly learning new things about the organization, being aware of industry trends and market factors, and routinely upgrading their skills and knowledge regarding their jobs.

Easy Come, Easy Go

A patron, intent on planning a special evening out with clients, asked the hostess at an upscale seafood restaurant when the restaurant intended to add its sushi bar. The hostess replied that she didn't know because the owners didn't tell her anything. The group went elsewhere.

Proactive Business Development

How many times have you passed up an opportunity to tell someone about who you are and what you do? Now, think about how many times your employees have passed up an opportunity to tell about who they are and where they work. As owners and managers, it is our responsibility to positively and proactively represent our organizations. Unfortunately, many employees in varying positions either don't know that this is their responsibility as well, or they don't take it very seriously. Employees need to know that proactive business development behaviors do not necessarily involve picking up the phone and making a cold call to a prospect. They can be conducted quite simply throughout the normal course of their jobs within their connections with suppliers, clients, and their community. And, they should realize that business development doesn't always apply to the actual sales of their company's products. Business development means positively and proactively representing the company and its image, which supports the organization's ability to recruit new employees.

Never Talk to Strangers?

A professional colleague tells the story about having worked in a bookstore while between jobs and liking everything about it. Kathy said that each customer's passion about certain topics caught on, prompting her to read more books that she wouldn't otherwise read. She sold more books as a result. Kathy also found herself outside of work, talking about the books and all the information to which she was exposed. One time, she remembers having talked about a recent "read" to a stranger while in line at the grocery store. The next day, she was surprised to see the "stranger" at the bookstore, buying the book for her husband! Kathy believes she's more successful influencing her company's demanding employee recruitment efforts in her position as traffic manager at a large chemical company as a result of what she learned at the bookstore. "I realized that everyone could be a potential employee, and I am positive when discussing what I do for a living," Kathy said.

The ASK WHY Model™

Before embarking on any BDEB initiative, you must first clarify performance expectations of yourself and your employees, and the way you do this is to ask the right kinds of questions. What performance do you seek in your employees in the finance department? Purchasing? Manufacturing? What specific behaviors or actions are you looking for? How will you know it when you see it? Who do you need this particular performance from—every employee in that department or select employees? Equally as important, what are things that you need to change about yourself as a manager? With these questions, you will specifically define the *desired performance* that will bring about the BDEB performance you are seeking.

You must evaluate and manage performance on an *individual* level, not among several individuals in the same position or department. This is important! Evaluating a group of employees is like comparing your children—each kid and employee has a unique personality and approach to dealing with people and situations within their comfort zone. One communications strategy may work wonders for employee X who works in the warehouse, for example, when the same communications strategy falls flat for employee Y who works in administration. (You may only have to give a stern look to child X while being sent to his room with no dinner works to curb child Y's urge to misbehave only temporarily!) While we all have organizational goals such as employee retention and customer satisfaction, it is individuals who do the work. And, remember the impact each individual has on organizational success. Just like clients and children, you must treat employees as individuals, each with a unique set of characteristics, talents, and needs. Then, and only then, can you reap the benefits from opportunities gained with a BDEB culture.

A statement that could easily be inserted into every employee's job description for almost any company is our definition of business development: *"Positively and proactively represent yourself and your company to everyone with whom you come in contact."* Remember the Five Groups of Influence™? Positively and proactively representing yourself and your company to everyone means to fellow employees, prospects, clients, suppliers, and to the community at large. If we plan to hold all employees accountable for implementing this principle, we must provide the necessary performance support that will enable them to do their best work.

After you have clarified the performance you seek, you must then understand what influences performance in your organization. Based on what the job is, there are certain competencies required to do that job. Use the ASK WHY Model™ to gain a better understanding of what it is really going to take to get the results you desire. Then, use this new information to help you integrate BDEB roles and responsibilities into your existing job or position descriptions.

The ASK WHY Model™ is a question-focused model that can take you as deep as you want to go to gather information about virtually anything. It was developed with the belief that people are much more likely to get positive results when they ask the right kinds of questions to determine why things exist as they are.

The ASK WHY Model™ will give you **permission** to look at the whole situation surrounding employee performance. You will be much more comfortable because you will be able to see the big picture and actually have proof that performance is impacted by a lot more than just the employee's behavior.

Before you can properly define success factors for your employees, you will need to examine your own success factors. That's why we recommend that you do a basic inventory of yourself in your role as owner and manager. Then, you can do an inventory of the various employee groups within your organization. This takes time, but it's time well spent since the outcome will be a well-defined list of job roles and success indicators for BDEB as well as for productive working behaviors in general. Chances are, this is an area of the business where you have needed more clarity anyway.

Attitudes   What are the attitudes you seek for this job role?

Skills   What skills are necessary for this job role?

Knowledge   What does this person need to know in order to perform this job role?

What are the work environment issues that impact employee performance?

How does the work this employee does impact the organization?

Your employee s motivation for improvement?

So, congratulations! You have just been given permission to ASK WHY! Before you begin your mission, (should you choose to accept it), you must fully understand what each letter in the ASK WHY Model™ represents. The following documentation should begin your adventure into the discovery of things about your organization that will brighten your way to a BDEB culture. (This part of the book will *not* self destruct.)

A S K WH Y
Attitude

Webster's Dictionary defines the word attitude as a posture or mental position. Tom Peters puts attitude right up there with service. In his series of books, *Reinventing Work: Professional Service Firm 50*, Peters says that if you want clients to return and buy again, your service—as well as—your attitude had better be good.

Attitude is one of the most important things that contributes to a successful organization. Yet, it's one of the hardest to teach. You can teach employees new skills for working, and you can educate them about your company and create a knowledge repository for easy information retrieval. But it is very hard to train employees on the attitudes necessary for good business. Existing attitudes about the company will best be changed when management in the company begins demonstrating a truly changed expectation.

If, in the past, you have not widely shared information and responsibility with employees, you can't expect a simple declaration to automatically change things. It just doesn't work like that. Since you have been conducting business the "old way" for years, you will have to prove that things are really different and you value these new behaviors. Give it time. BDEB is not a program; it's a philosophy that should be around for a long time. It will be worth the time it takes to bring people along naturally.

Once employees realize that you mean what you say and you are obviously going to support their information and performance development needs on a long-term basis, they will come around. Changes in attitude occur when people truly feel supported and valued. You have to earn them. And, there are some people who simply won't change. That is why you must define the attitudes you expect in your new BDEB culture, and make them a part of new employees' job descriptions and performance expectations. Consider these attitudes while making future hiring decisions.

What are some attitudes that make you a high performing manager? Some possible answers include: High morale, confidence (I can do it), strong work ethic, loyalty, sincere helpfulness, responsible, responsive, and positive. What are some attitudes of a high performing BDEB employee? A good starting list is: Sincere helpfulness, positivity, empathy, respectfulness, trustworthiness, and honesty. Statement number one on the BDEB Skills Assessment— "I say thank you"—is an indicator of an attitudinal factor. When someone has an attitude of thankfulness, they shine brightly as someone people feel good about being around. There is a statistic in public speaking that 99% of people in an audience, for example, want the speaker to be successful. The same could be said about our customers and friends, and when we show our genuine thankfulness for their business and referrals, we perpetuate more of the same.

The Power of Our Beliefs

Attitude is also an important player in employees' ability to abandon the "business development is not my job" mentality. Let's face it. You're going to meet with resistance from those employees who believe that business development is simply "selling" in disguise. So let's talk about selling for a minute.

Making a contribution to the business development effort depends on each of your employees examining their current belief system around "selling." Selling in an organization isn't really much different than selling in everyday life. The problem is that we have built a wall around "sales" as we perceive it, and we let it guide our outlook. If you think about it, it is true. We sell many things to others --our philosophy for living, our work ethic, how we raise our children, how we contribute to society, our value system. We are always selling in some form. The only difference is, we don't recognize these things as selling because they come *naturally* to us, and they're easy, as a result.

Those who haven't chosen a career in sales perceive selling as hard. Harry Bullis, former chairman of the board of General Mills, positions selling as a natural extension of helping others. He used to tell his salespeople to "forget about the sales you hope to make and concentrate on the service you want to render." Bullis says that if each salesperson would start out each morning with the thought, "I want to help as many people as possible today," instead of "I want to make as many sales as possible today," they would find a more easy and open approach to their buyers, and they would make more sales. This same principle applies to all employees, not just sales-people. Bullis says, "The person who goes out to help people to a happier and easier way of life is exercising the highest type of sales-manship."

Ask employees in various job functions to give you a word or phrase that they associate with sales. Depending on the employee's job role, you might get words such as "cold calling," annoying," "telemarketing calls during dinner," and "pressure." Others might say "flexibility," "company car," and "commission." Put it to the test. What word comes to *your* mind when you think of the word sales? These ideas are really our underlying **beliefs** about the sales function. The word "belief" is defined as "the conviction that something is true." The power of our beliefs can push us to accomplish or hold us back from doing the things we truly want or need to do. Here is an example:

Beliefs "Shape" Our Ability to Reach Goals

A group of 20 women who had lost weight before but gained it back multiple times were members in a weight loss program. During one class, the women were asked to raise their hand if they believed they would lose five pounds in the next month. All 20 women raised their hand. They were then asked to raise their hand if they believed they would reach their goal weight. About 10 women raised their hand. Finally, they were asked to raise their hand if they believed that when they reached their goal weight, they would be able to keep the weight off. No one raised her hand.

This story demonstrates how our beliefs can shape our attitudes. It also demonstrates how our beliefs can block progress. It isn't just about having a belief, but it is how we let that belief influence us that matters. Going back to our definition of business development, employees who simply adopt an attitude to positively and proactively represent themselves and their company to everyone with whom they come in contact can indeed influence business development. The point is that we can each achieve great things for our organizations with an attitude that we can have an influence on business development.

A S K W H Y
Skill

A skill is the ability to do something well especially as the result of long practical experience. Skills can be taught in many ways including on-the-job training, modeling, simulation, practice, and trial and error.

Think about some of the specific skills that make you a high performing owner or manager. You probably have some technical expertise or you wouldn't be in a leadership position. Hopefully, you possess some soft skills such as good time management, interpersonal, and communications skills. Perhaps you have worked your way up in the industry and organization and now possess job specific skills that enable you to teach others to do their jobs.

How did you rate yourself on statement number 18 on the BDEB Skills Assessment? Mentoring is hard to master and requires the mentor's genuine interest in the employee being mentored. It's also a skill that is desirable for BDEB. A BDEB culture will create additional opportunities for trial and error. From a management standpoint, it will be important for managers in your organization to master the ability to help each lesson learned become an opportunity for growth and not a deterrent for BDEB.

A starting list of the employee skills necessary for a BDEB culture include:

- Good communication skills
- Information gathering: Questioning & Listening
- Information sharing: Report and proposal writing (or good knowledge of what it takes to make an effective proposal)
- Informal and/or formal presentation skills
- Networking
- Problem solving
- Time management
- Ability to see the big picture

A BDEB culture also requires skills in making and keeping the natural connections that you make daily in both your professional job and your personal life. Teaching this skill to employees might be a little bit more difficult, because you must first convince them of their importance in the business development effort. The use of the company's information bite discussed in Principle 1 will go a long way toward helping employees develop the skill necessary for leveraging their connections.

A S **K** W H Y

Knowledge

Knowledge is defined as the state of knowing, cognition, or understanding. The basic difference between knowledge and information is in a person's acceptance of the message. You can have information provided to you about a specific concept, and you can turn around and provide that information to someone else. Only when this information becomes understood does it truly become knowledge.

What specific knowledge do you need to be a high performing owner or manager? The list is remarkably the same for employees and is reflected in many of the statements on the BDEB Skills Assessment:

- Knowledge about your company
- Product knowledge
- Knowledge about your job
- Knowledge about the industry
- Knowledge about your personal strengths and weaknesses
- Knowledge about the customer
- Knowledge about your company's sales and marketing strategies, systems, and goals
- Knowledge about selling your company's products and services

The most successful learning depends on understanding what you are to do, then practicing until you can apply what you have learned.

Adults make a *conscious* decision about what they are willing to learn and what they are not willing to learn. One of the first tasks of the adult educator is to develop a "need to know" in the learners. If a training program or an on-the-job learning experience is to be fully effective, the learners need to see clearly how what is being taught will benefit them and fulfill a "felt need" in them.

Helping Adults Learn New Things

It may be helpful for you to understand that adults prefer to take in information in different ways. Some prefer to hear the message. They have an **auditory** learning preference. With these people, you must tell them what you want them to know. Some prefer to see the message. They have a **visual** learning preference. This group benefits greatly from the use of visuals like a multi-media presentation, handouts, charts and graphs, and other visual tools. Still others need to try things out and get a feeling for things. These people have a **kinesthetic** learning preference. They prefer to learn by doing. A great exercise to accelerate learning with this group is to have them do some type of activity with their hands. You can significantly increase learning potential among your staff by accommodating all three ways to learn while communicating your important organizational messages.

Another important premise about adult learning is the adult learning cycle. By understanding this cycle and building its considerations into your training and development efforts, you can expect better results. The adult learning cycle is simply the process we all go through when we learn something new. The cycle is dynamic; adults will continue to collect information on these subjects and synthesize it for usefulness and relevance. The first phase of the

143

adult learning cycle is the **information** phase. Adults learn by being informed especially when the "teacher" first considers all three primary learning styles

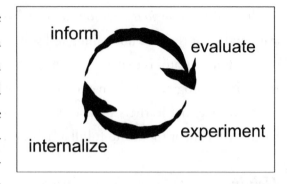

(auditory, visual, kinesthetic) and uses appropriate teaching methodologies that support each learner's style. The next phase is **evaluation**. Adults always evaluate what they are hearing compared to existing knowledge and skills on the subject. That's why it is important to design training tactics that facilitate these comparisons. As adults receive and evaluate more information, they begin to **experiment** with the new knowledge. A critical part of this phase is to provide safe environments for adults to experiment with the new knowledge or skill. Unfortunately, many people cut this component out of training environments for the sake of saving time, money, and resources. When there has been enough information and time for evaluation and experimentation, adults will incorporate the new skills and knowledge into their routines by **internalizing** their new knowledge.

One, Two, Cha-Cha-Cha

To fully understand the adult learning cycle, let's learn something new. . . such as ballroom dancing! First, an instructor must show you the moves and techniques and teach you how to do them. Therefore, you must first become *informed.* As you watch the instructor demonstrate the dance moves, your mind is taking everything in and *evaluating* each move in relation to your current skills and dance capabilities. Perhaps you think, "I could do that!" (Perhaps not). Either way, you try it, and you practice your new techniques. You *experiment* with these techniques and others to establish your own style.

Before long, you're doing it! You're ballroom dancing, and you're getting good results. You're having fun, getting some exercise, and most importantly, you don't look like a goof. You can't remember when you didn't know how to ballroom dance. You've *internalized* your new skills.

A S K WH Y

What are the work environment issues that impact employee performance?

Your work environment is anything that has an influence, either positive or negative, on your ability to do your work. You could work in an environment that allows roller-blading in the halls to inspire creativity. . .or you could work in cubicles. Your work area could be cluttered in spite of the fact that others often need to retrieve information from your office. Or, you may have ample wall space and use it to post motivational posters and corporate goals to inspire BDEB performance.

Your work environment should provide you with the tools, supplies, and performance support you need to do your best work or at least to the formal performance standards. Do you have the tools and resources needed to do your job? What information-sharing systems are in place to effectively communicate information to all employees? What are the incentives and the disincentives inherent in the work environment that impact your ability to do your best work?

A S K W**H**Y

**How does the work this employee does
impact the organization?**

Can you demonstrate how your performance links to critical business factors such as sales, profits, and customer retention? If you weren't employed at your company, would they have to replace you? What is your contribution? How do you add value?

A good exercise to do would be to have all employees answer this question for their own job functions: What different things do they do on a daily basis that can either be directly or indirectly linked to your organization's profits? For example, a professional peer says that she adds value by training operators in her company to help them reduce the number of mistakes. As a result, operators were able to perform tasks correctly, preventing an actual $50,000 factory loss. The company benefited because it now has an additional $50,000 that went directly to the bottom line.

Some other possible "revelations" could include:

- I help make clients happy so they keep buying our products/services.
- I develop goodwill for my company in the community so we leverage our advertising and marketing dollars.
- I process orders in a timely fashion for faster delivery so we have more capacity.
- I answer customer and employee questions to support the sales team.
- I keep the machinery running smoothly for less down time.
- I return all phone calls promptly so people have a positive impression of our organization.

Employees who understand what they are doing within their everyday work can have an impact the bottom line. Understanding personal impact encourages employee retention, facilitates exceptional customer satisfaction, enables a better ability to promote within the ranks, promotes better negotiating skills, and highlights the natural connections for business development opportunities.

A S K WHY

Your motivation for improvement?

People are motivated for different reasons. For example, some people request training because someone in their organization handed down an ultimatum: Help our people manage their time better! Or, perhaps a new competitor has moved into your market and you want to retain your strong customer base. Or, the survival of the business is on the line.

What is your motivation for improvement? What might be some reasons why employees are motivated to improve? Some employees may be motivated by pay raise and profit sharing plans. They may work best by receiving bonuses based on the performance of the company. This has worked well for many companies that have taken time to educate employees on how to read the company's income statements. That way, employees can track their performance with that of the company's, and they can understand what needs to happen for them to get their bonus.

Employees may be motivated by the fact that their job is secure as long as they constantly seek to improve themselves and look for new ways to perform better. Still other employees take pride in their work and are motivated to improve for the simple reason that self-improvement means higher value as an employee. You can tell these employees from others in that they take the time to ask for frequent and timely feedback in order to improve their skills and attitude.

As managers, it is very important to take the time to learn what motivates employees. After all, what works for one employee may not work for another, and issuing blanket rewards for performance standards may result in a massive waste of your time. People are motivated differently. Knowing that a pay raise is in store for a job well done may be the motivation needed for an employee to succeed. Others might simply take pride in their work and a job well done. Still others need recognition from their peers or supervisors.

Converting your existing culture into a BDEB culture will not happen overnight. Using the ASK WHY Model™ will go far, however, in helping you lay a strong foundation for employee support and participation in positively and proactively representing your business to everyone.

Putting Principle 5 Into Action

To successfully incorporate a BDEB environment within your organization, you must work with both managers and employees separately to develop necessary BDEB skills. The following are action ideas broken into the two groups for Managers and Employees.

Action Ideas for Managers

 Remember, it is important that managers model the attitudes and behaviors required for a BDEB environment. Determine the business development skill level of senior management by using high performing business development managers as a benchmark for performance. To do this, first select a manager who has been a successful contributor to business development. Following the ASK WHY Model™, go down the list of questions and answer them with that particular manager in mind. Interview him if necessary. Then, look at the other managers and determine specific areas that could use improvement. Once it has been determined what skills require improvement, provide appropriate direction, tools, and training.

 Create a tool for senior managers to help them plan their time and direct their activities around business development. Use the BDEB Skills Assessment if necessary. This particular assessment can be modi-

fied to fit your specific culture and should be used as a guide to help you select high payoff business development activities. Remember, the goal is to spend some of your time in proactive business development activities. Incorporating your organization's Channels of Opportunity™ highlights will make this action richer. Middle managers should be reporting their <u>proactive</u> and <u>reactive</u> business development activities to senior managers.

 Have all employees, especially senior management, go through a class on building relationships and business potential. Create an informal "discovery guide" to highlight the types of information they need to be capturing to develop future business prospects.

Action Ideas for Employees

 Copy the BDEB Skills Assessment from the Appendix of this book, and ask employees to take it. If you discover that some of the ideas involve management support, find ways to give it to them! For employees, these ideas are too important to ignore and could mean the difference between whether or not they are valued in the organization. And finally, to develop specific staff development objectives for business development, we suggest you pull from the "I" statements and work with each employee to develop a personal action/goal plan.

Create an online corporate learning environment, if possible, and give all employees access. Employees will then have the opportunity to review training modules and tips sheets for key business development principles within the company. Incorporate your own BDEB "teachable points of view." A teachable point of view is a fact based on your company and its experience in selling its products and services. If you worked out your Channels of Opportunity™ in Principle 3, you probably have several nuggets of wisdom to share regarding successful ways to add to your customer list. This information is typically something that can be readily shared and translated to different job functions throughout the company.

Provide each employee with some type of job description or role clarity and an explanation as to how they will be evaluated. Never hire an employee without clear expectations in place and expect her to help design her own job description. This is a recipe for trouble and could cause tension and conflict later if she's not living up to your previously undefined expectations.

Recognize employee business development contributions! This is important! Know where your business comes from and who might have made the first connection or influenced the sale. Many times the sales person gets all the credit for having closed the business when perhaps that sales person learned of the lead through another employee not directly involved in sales. Track this. Know when this occurs. Never ignore the contributions of employee influencers, but applaud their efforts in a corporate newsletter or memo, openly recognizing them for their contributions.

ACTION Keep the employee in the loop. When an employee brings a business lead to the table, don't just say thank you and hand it to a sales person for follow up. Keep the employee in the loop so they know where the lead went. Chances are that they might have additional contact with the prospect. When employees are kept in the loop, they are better able to seek the kinds of meaningful information that could win a deal, be more informed in front of customers, and share in the excitement of new business. For example, Odetics, a company based in Anaheim, California, shares important information with all employees by announcing news of a new contract over the company's public address system. They also share their earnings information in the company newspaper.

ACTION Make sure all employees know when your company receives any publicity. Provide copies of the PR. Make sure all employees know your marketing and advertising strategies. And, make sure they know about any special offers your company has out there.

On a Sam's Club rebate program form, the company asks the question, "How many unplanned items did you purchase as a result of this promotion?" Think of the opportunity for additional business if every single Sam's Club employee told ten of their closest friends and family about the sale. And, think of the dollars that result if every one of those ten individuals purchased two or more things they hadn't planned for!

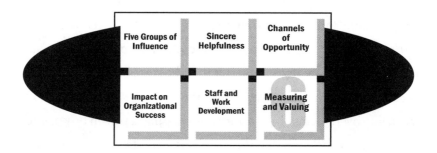

Principle 6

**Valuing a variety of business development
activities and results improves outcomes.**

Up to this point, we have discussed the benefits of:

- Maximizing your natural connections with the Five
  Groups of Influence™
- Encouraging an environment of sincere helpfulness
- Knowing and leveraging your organization's primary
  Channels of Opportunity™
- Understanding and appreciating each employee's impact
  on the organization
- Ongoing development of both staff and work environ-
  ment

155

In this chapter, we want to show you how important it is to truly *value* BDEB performance. You are ready to learn how valuing and measuring a variety of business development activities performed by employees will improve business development outcomes.

Our individual beliefs, values, and goals often dictate what we value. People value something when they feel they have received a fair return for something exchanged. For example, a person might buy brand name catsup despite the fact that the store brand is $2.00 less because he likes its taste over that of the lower cost item. He values its quality over pricing. In consumer purchasing, a person buys something when he believes that the price was a good value for the quality or quantity he received. So, how do you place a value on what might be considered soft-return investments? How do you truly value an investment of say, $800 on one employee's membership and active participation in an organization if you don't see a direct return immediately? When we talk about valuing something, we're suggesting that you overcome the urge to judge BDEB activities before they've had a chance to pay off long term. And, in this example, we're making the assumption that participation in this particular organization represents one of your Channels of Opportunity™.

Managers are often valued by how happy and productive their direct reports are. Companies with employee satisfaction and production goal attainment measures in place can routinely study data to see how managers are doing. Salespeople are valued by some pretty hard evidence, too—sales! In fact, commissioned sales people receive constant validation that their activities are paying off for their company by the size of their paychecks. Why couldn't it be this easy for the rest of us? One obstacle to overcome is the perception that the *only* activities that contribute to business development are the obvious ones such as the number of winning proposals, successful sales calls, and qualified leads generated.

Closers and Influencers

When BDEB becomes an important part of your work culture, you will begin to see two types of employee emerge: the "closers" and the "influencers." The closers are those people who relentlessly go for the business. They are fearless when it comes to asking for the sale and are quite comfortable calling on prospects until they agree to buy. Not easily intimidated, "closers" tend to be more aggressive and goal-oriented. Obviously, organizations want closers because they have a great impact on securing new business. Sales guru and author, Robert Shook says that in the sales profession "your number one objective as a salesperson is to close sales."

Yet, closing is cited as one of the tasks in which salespeople have the most difficulty. Because of its importance in the sales cycle, lots of focus is given to the topic of closing. Books are written on the subject, providing hungry salespeople with ideas for effective closing techniques. In Tom Hopkins book, *How to Master the Art of Selling*, he provides numerous techniques for closing the business based on his proven experience as a lifetime salesman. Closers who aren't in a sales role within an organization are those individuals who tend to gravitate towards positions in collections, customer service, sales of tangible products. Ministers, educators, counselors, and police officers can be "closers" depending on their styles and situations.

"Influencers," on the other hand, are important in the overall sales cycle as well. Influencers are those individuals who influence public perceptions about your products and services in many ways. They are confident in answering questions and discussing products and services in a non-threatening (sales) manner. Malcolm Gladwell in his book, *The Tipping Point*, calls these individuals "connectors."

Influencers are referral artists. An influencer might say something like, "You ought to check out our new line of skin care products. I tried them as soon as they came out and immediately fell in love." The influencer says no more about the product line during the exchange, but a sale has been influenced when some time in the future that person buys one of the products in the line.

Valuing the characteristics and actions of these individuals becomes a tricky prospect indeed. It's very easy to assign a value to closers since sales can be directly traced to their actions throughout an often-documented transaction process. When we talk about 100% employee involvement, we are largely suggesting that employees develop the ability to become influential in the overall business development process. By considering themselves influencers of your products and services, employees can be prepared by regularly updating their product knowledge and looking for ways to suggest additional items when customers and prospects hint at needs during non-sales-related interactions. Here is a story that illuminates the dichotomy between closers and influencers in your organization and how placing a value on each style is so important.

Who Gets Credit?

As a new member of a local Kiwanis club, I enjoyed telling people about how wonderful it was to be included in a community of people who were dedicated to serving others. During a phone call from Harry Bensen, a professional seeking to network with our company, I learned that he had been a Kiwanian at another chapter and was interested in rejoining. He now lived in the area so I casually suggested he come to one of our weekly meetings. During the conversation, Harry mentioned that he frequented a local coffee shop so I suggested he look up George and Diana Callahan, other Kiwanians who also frequently visited the coffee shop.

The next morning at Kiwanis, George Callahan stood up and introduced his guest—Harry Bensen, the man I'd spent an hour on the phone with the day before! George proceeded to tell the story about how he was at Java Junction the day before and was approached by Harry who said he overhead his name and thought he'd introduce himself. Harry told George that I had coincidentally mentioned his name on the phone that morning. During their visit, George sold him on the benefits of our club and invited Harry to Kiwanis as his guest. Harry, in turn, joined our Kiwanis club the next morning.

Members get credit by the national Kiwanis organization for recruiting new members. Credit for Harry's membership went to George Callahan as it should have. After all, George closed the business. And, when George stood up and publicly acknowledged how the transaction began, I was satisfied knowing that I'd had a small part as an "influencer" in the sale.

As unlikely as it sounds, this stuff happens all of the time! Opportunities present themselves constantly and when employees are properly prepared to be positive and proactive ambassadors for their organization, they are likely influencers of sales made later when a salesperson closes the business. The potential for trouble comes in when credit is given and at no time in the process was it documented that an employee influenced the sale. Closers reap rewards in terms of credits or commissions for having made the sale, and influencers should have recognition for having done their part in the overall sales process. And, that's probably all these people need, because frankly, most influencers are relieved that someone else can close the business they find and influence. Pats on the back are nice. Recognition is divine. The bottom line is that, in a BDEB culture, valuing employees who influence business development will suddenly become very important to perpetuate the behaviors that lead to new business.

Valuing the Cost of BDEB

Have you ever implemented a new business approach or training class only to see its momentum dissolve months later? Measurement is a topic of much debate, especially in the training industry. For example, it can be hard to place a dollar value on improved soft skills. Buyers of training want to see a monetary return because they know what they spent for the training. Sometimes managers get excited about the expected outcomes, but pull back their support when they aren't seeing a return on their investment as soon as they'd like. Rather, they should be analyzing the performance using the ASK WHY Model™ to determine what else needs to happen in order to get the desired performance. This lack of management support for a new training initiative or operating procedure often leads to a "flavor of the month" practice. Or, changing an existing culture becomes an overwhelming challenge when middle managers, who are often tasked by *their* managers with the change directive, lose sight of the goals. (They may not have even shared the same goals or vision to begin with!)

The Softer Side of Business Development

What might be some softer investments in business development for your organization? Participation in trade associations? Inclusion of all employees in company status and planning meetings? Subscriptions to magazines, industry resource materials, and business books? Company-wide orientations and routine information distribution? Consider these activities and the estimated costs associated with them. Keep in mind that some of the activities you are considering aren't necessarily new investments. Some activities might be worth getting more involved with especially if your Channels of Opportunity™ suggest expanding these investments.

Participation in trade associations.

We use trade associations as an example because this is an area in which many industries already invest. In many organizations, though, it's common for just the salespeople and managers to actively participate. Rarely will you find front line employees attending these meetings. If your Channels of Opportunity™ point to an association as a viable opportunity for business development, it might make sense to involve a larger number of employees. Granted, you're going to have an increased cost in meeting fees if more people are going to participate. In the spirit of BDEB, you recognize that the involvement creates more opportunities for employees to learn first-hand knowledge of industry issues as well as make additional business development connections with their Five Groups of Influence™. Factor in investments including membership and meeting fees, as well as time spent away from work for *active* association participation.

Company-wide status and planning meetings.

There are always a handful of employees who are not included in status and planning meetings within a company. That's not to say that many organizations do not value the input of these employees; rather, they don't attend these meetings because of their job responsibilities and the fact that they may not deal directly with clients, prospects, and/or suppliers. While rotating through these meetings, employees who work in varying positions are given the opportunity to learn more about the business from these decision-making and strategy sessions. The investment here is the cost of time spent away from their regular job responsibilities.

Subscriptions to magazines, industry resource materials, and the purchase of business books.

Obviously, if employees are going to be more involved and connecting more, they will have more opportunities to share what they can with others. We believe that keeping abreast of industry news and trends is an integral part of any employee's job. It gives them a wider perspective on issues as they relate to customers, and nurtures a brighter work environment. Learning through reading should always be on an employee's to-do list, if necessary, at the expense of another task. It is a minimal time investment of, say, one to two hours per week compared to the impact that new knowledge, and the confidence this knowledge instills. Plan on budgeting for multiple copies of the most popular publications depending on the number of employees in your organization.

Routine company-wide orientations and information distribution.

Not sharing critical business information is one of the biggest missed opportunities in businesses today. We believe that this is a very important activity—one that has a high return when done well. Organizations tend to value this activity more when they have a lot of new employees entering the company. Unfortunately, many companies do not invest in this area since it may involve hiring or subcontracting to create and maintain this routine information. In addition to the up-front cost of developing an orientation program, the ongoing cost of this activity shouldn't cost you much more than time spent away from regular job responsibilities. The cost is offset by enhanced employee performance.

As you can see from the BDEB activities mentioned above, there are specific costs associated with each activity. And, each activity should create value for the organization in the form of business development results. Consider basing your budget on your Channels of Opportunity™, your unique business connections, the number of your employees, and the type of products and/or services you sell. The goal is to maximize your connections to the Five Groups of Influence™.

Budgeting for Business Development

Professional service firms often have business development activities for all associates and partners built into their operating budgets. An associate at a large law firm in Indianapolis is given a yearly $2,000 marketing budget to use for entertaining clients, philanthropic contributions, and memberships. He is given $2,500 a year for continuing professional education as he sees fit.

To gain the outcomes from implementing a BDEB culture—increased profits, higher employee morale, and more promotional opportunities—you must learn how to measure the softer side against your "hard" business measures by focusing less on the dollars spent and more on the outcomes from those dollars spent. You can begin the process of developing your own budget by evaluating your existing activities and expenses and expanding them based on your Channels of Opportunity™. Then, you will get a good idea of how you can budget for costs associated with creating a BDEB culture in your organization. Once you've eliminated the surprise, you can begin to focus more of your attention on following up with employees to discover results. Look for:

- Information employees are gathering about clients and prospects
- Potential for add-on project work and/or referral business;
- Prospects previously unidentified by sales staff
- Information that can be summarized and shared with other employees
- Employees who emerge as natural "closers"
- Employees who emerge as natural "influencers" who have gone the extra mile to proactively represent the company

Establishing Mutual Trust

As owners and managers, your role is to be supportive of employees who opt to participate in trade associations, read industry journals, and participate more fully in the business. In order for these activities to be successful, *mutual trust* must exist between managers and employees. Managers must trust employees as they perform activities that may lead to the discovery of business development opportunities. Some of these activities may require employees to leave their jobs for an hour or two, and managers must trust that the employees have the company's best interests in mind. This trust can be established at the very beginning of BDEB by clearly defining expectations and corporate goals with employees.

Conversely, employees must trust that managers will continue to support their BDEB efforts. They must remain confident that managers will show an interest in what they're doing and the information they are bringing to the table. Employees will continue to produce when they are given the latitude to make decisions on their own as to whether or not they should continue their involvement in a certain activity. Managers and employees should sit down prior to involvement in BDEB activities and agree upon a reasonable time frame for business development opportunities to emerge. And, we're not necessarily talking about leads, although obtaining more qualified leads is nice and is the ultimate goal! What we're saying is that business development opportunities include those moments when employees have an influence in creating positive awareness of your company in support of the sales function. The fact is that when employees are given the chance to shine, they will. Armed with the knowledge of where your prime business development connections are made, employees will choose to devote more time toward increasing the organization's exposure to your targeted Channels of Opportunity™. They will also exemplify the level of service and commitment that your organization endeavors to give to clients, professional peers, and employees.

Remember, the benefits of investing in many of these activities can be proven with routine analysis of your organization's Channels of Opportunity™. We suggest that you budget time to review the results of these efforts no less than once every three months to determine effectiveness and where extra time and support could be given to help employees seek and find business development opportunities.

Let's see how BDEB worked for the Jones Corporation. And remember, this could be you. . .

Once Upon a Time. . .

. . . there was a company owner who learned that his employees' connections with prospects, suppliers, clients, and the community were the best source of his company's business opportunities. (He had read the book, *Business Development is Everyone's Business*.)

Using the principles in the book as his guide, Frank decided to create a work environment that was supportive of his employees to use their natural connections to develop more business for the company. He encouraged active participation in industry associations and community business groups. He allowed his people time off with pay to participate in not-for-profit committees and other volunteer work. He sponsored in-house learning opportunities to increase employees' product and financial knowledge. He shared valuable information regarding the organization's financial position. And, he empowered employees to make more of their own decisions on-the-job.

Over the next few months, things began to change for the company. Employees were getting out more, meeting people, and representing the company well with their new knowledge and attitudes. As a result, over time, more

---

connections than usual began turning into genuine business leads for the company. Now that everyone in the organization knew where their business really came from, there was more of a focus on the top three Channels of Opportunity™. They were spending fewer resources chasing blue sky. And, they were delivering fewer proposals that took hours to prepare to prospects who were never going to buy.

Employees also seemed to be more helpful in general, recognizing that they were also each other's customers. There were times when people struggled a little in their new roles, but that was to be expected, and Frank did what he could to support the employees. He was encouraged to see that everyone in the organization could now articulate the impact that their role had on the company's bottom line. Because of his investments in his existing staff, Frank was indeed beginning to see evidence in the form of tangible results that the BDEB principles were prompting in his organization.

Then, Frank started hearing about a new technology within their industry that could make his company's products virtually obsolete within a year. He reacted by doing what many hardworking, business-minded company owners do. Deciding that product diversification was critical, he made plans to invest heavily in the new technology that would keep them in line with their competition.

Very similar to the onslaught of bad weather, Frank started battening down the hatches and cutting expenses in order to meet their research and development goals. He decided to discontinue "programs" that had previously supported BDEB. Training sessions, memberships, and meeting fees became expendable again. After all, he reasoned, these were "soft" investments in time, resources, and money, and he needed all of the resources he could get to weather out the coming storm.

Frank's employees were confused because suddenly support for the efforts that had seemed to matter just a short time before was taken away. They had seen the positive effects of their efforts in terms of connections made, enhanced customer service, and a collective team spirit. Now, they felt at a loss for how they could help the company in this time of need. And, because Frank had refocused his attention on developing this new technology, the employees saw less and less of him on the floor.

Frank caught wind of the negativity and tension within his company. He began noticing an increase in absenteeism and learned that several people were thinking about leaving the company. He couldn't figure it out! Here he was, trying to create a new product that would save the company, and employees were bailing out for what seemed like calmer seas!

One day, while Frank was sitting at his desk, head down

in financial reports, a small voice spoke to him. He looked around his office, confused, expecting to see his very own fantasy business guru (clearly, he had read his share of story-type business books.) Frank realized where the voice came from—his conscience. He turned to his laptop and began to write:

In my effort to streamline and make preparations for new advancements in technology, I have missed a critical step. I have forgotten to utilize my best resource. I have not included my employees who are obviously interested in seeing the company prosper and who are now worried about the security of their jobs. Had I really valued the BDEB activities and their subsequent results on the company, would I have still cut back the things that I did?

Now that I think about it, I remember how this felt many years ago when I worked for another metal fabrication company. When I could, I worked hard to make the right kinds of connections, and, as a result, I gathered valuable information and market insights that directed my efforts. When I shared what I had learned with management, though, they acted like they didn't care and refused to listen to my ideas for change. Why did they pay me to positively and proactively represent my company if they weren't going to listen to what I was learning from my connections? No wonder I felt undervalued, threatened, and resentful. Eventually I left.

But now the tables are turned and I'm "management." And, here I've done the same type of thing to my people. I'm now realizing that technology alone will not keep this company on track. We need the active involvement of all employees, our clients, and suppliers. The community will be the source of our new clients.

I must write out my goals for this company. What do I want? What do we need to do to meet these challenges? Whose help do I need?

Frank's fingers flew over the keys. The ideas were coming faster than he could type! He began to outline plans to call a company-wide meeting to ask for employees' help and support to meet the challenges ahead. He developed a list of the internal resources that he would personally ask to be on a development task force—employees who represented a cross section of the departments within the company. He made a commitment to reinstate BDEB activities, allowing all employees to continue their community involvement. After all, he reasoned, does it make sense to close off from the world at a time when you need access to resources and new customers?

Frank had realized a basic truth for the success of his organization. By implementing a BDEB culture, he was enabling his employees to perform a lot of indirect business development activities. But, he shouldn't judge his business success only on what he saw in his company's financial reports. His goal was to get these basic business development attitudes and behaviors mainstreamed in his corporate culture.

Frank made several copies of this document, called a management meeting, and gave the copies to all of his managers to enlist their support and ideas. He remembered another business truth that he'd read somewhere— something about "we manage what we measure." Using hints from a book he'd read called *The Talent Solution*, Frank scheduled a work session with his management team to create a "balanced portfolio for measuring results" that included different areas of his business.

The managers agreed they should continue to enhance systems for measuring traditional factors or lagging indicators such as total revenue and profitability. But after a while, Joe, the Production Manager had an idea. He showed the rest of the managers his notes and said, "We measure these lagging indicators in my department. If we could work backward from these and begin to identify some leading indicators that get us this, we're on our way to establishing comprehensive BDEB performance indicators for our company. After all, if we spend all of our time measuring the end results, it seems to me that we're not measuring progress as it occurs."

The Vice President of Sales agreed. "Joe's right! I think that if we were to list in order of importance what we think our company values most, we might be interested and surprised to see how the list compares to what our company actually measures. For example, we say that we're all about customer service, and we even have a client satisfaction rating system to measure how we're doing. Yet, all we really reward is volume sales, not the quality of the sale or even the service rendered. Sometimes I think we get so focused on making the next deal, we're not as focused on all the details of customer service. Quantity does not necessarily mean quality."

The Quality Manager said, "We learned a hard lesson several years ago when we implemented TQM (total quality management), remember that? Remember how we were looking at how to get more quality out of our systems, and we found that we were only rewarding quantity?" He shook his head and laughed. "We were asking the question, how do we get more out of staff, equipment, systems, processes, etc. The result—speed—produced more errors, which cost more in the long run. The reality was that we were getting more of what we asked for, but less of what our original intention was: quality!"

After much discussion, they wrapped up the work session and went back to their areas. Their task was to write their own unique list of departmental performance benchmarks before their next work session. During that time, Frank learned that the new product team was making great development progress. He was pleased (and relieved) that he had assembled a team that included more people than just his engineers.

His conscience spoke to him again about a week following the managers work session. This time, Frank was out on the shop floor, reviewing some client drawings. He could tell that he needed to write down what was on his mind, so he quickly finished what he was doing and went to his office.

"What are the top concerns that company owners have of running a profitable business?" he thought to himself. Frank wasn't surprised that he'd been thinking about this, because deep down he was worried about the changes that were happening within his company. Changes, which while exciting, were still intimidating in the scope of their challenge. Frank began to write:

- I'm worried about our financial situation especially during this time of development.
- I'm worried that our customers will decide to go elsewhere until we can get this new technology completed.
- I'm worried about being able to recruit good people to work in my company.
- I'm worried that we aren't really sharing the lessons that we've learned over the years. It seems like we've been doing the same things over and over again which gets us nowhere.

Frank studied his list of concerns and had an idea. He thought, "We should come up with performance benchmarks that meet the needs of these issues!" He wrote down four key areas and began brainstorming things that they might try to measure within their organization.

Frank took his list with him to the next managers work session that week. He began to tell them how he came up with his list. "I was thinking the other day about how worried I was about a few things around here when I realized that I wasn't the only owner who was concerned about

Performance Benchmarks

Financial Performance
Profit margins, Gross revenues, Cash flow security, Number of prospects, Inventory turns, Variable expenses, Number of qualified leads, Number of current customers, Number of referrals, Backlog, Number of opportunities for target audience exposure

Customers
Product and customer development? How satisfied following proposal process? How satisfied during and following the project? Has client been able to track evidence of benefits of our work? Do we ask for or receive written testimonials from clients? Do we respond to negative client feedback? Do our clients refer business to us? Does the project team meet the needs of the client? Do we know what the client expects? Are we meeting our deadlines?

Human Resources
Recruiting, Retention, Staff development, Meeting personal goals, Supporting organization goals, Continual learning, Staff contributions, Company and product knowledge, Plans made and budgets established for work force development, Managers are held accountable for supporting staff development, Corporate Image, Professional Peers, Proactive business development activities, Value-added contribution, Presenting self

Knowledge Management
Facility Utilization, Number of times I used the organization's information bite this week, Corporate memory (lessons learned), Testing employees' abilities to engage the organization's information bite, Communication strategies, Opportunity database management, Account profiles, Five Groups of Influence™

these things. In fact, I was talking with another owner last week and he mentioned some of the same concerns."

"If we're truly going to have a BDEB culture and be able to mainstream certain behaviors into employees' job roles, we need to know that our overall organization's goals are being met. That's why I created this list of things that we typically measure and included some things that we should be measuring if we're going to be successful at getting 100% employee involvement."

The managers were excited and enthusiastically agreed to the list. They included their measures and came up with a master document for performance measurement. The HR and Marketing Managers agreed to work together with the list to enhance employees' job descriptions, outlining the activities that formally and informally contribute to business and product development based on each individual employee's job role. Frank reasoned that it was important for the two to work together on this task to blend existing performance measures according to job role with business development behaviors and activities based on job function.

From that, the HR Manager began developing a performance evaluation system based on tasks, goals, and measurement of goals achieved. She remembered a time when a former boss of hers, after she had produced and implemented a successful training session for her co-workers, came up to her and said, "I appreciate you." That simple remark went a long way toward encouraging her to work even harder for that company!

"As employees develop new skills and discard old ones, it is necessary to rewrite job descriptions so that the human resource department knows how to recruit in the future and how to evaluate and reward current employees. Because the workflow has changed, standards by which employees are measured must change as well."

In planning a performance evaluation system, the HR Manager considered the fact that humans thrive on regular reminders that what they are doing is important and appreciated.

The HR Manager then wondered what to do when employees have proven themselves to be valuable contributors to business development within the company. A friend recommended she read the book by Bob Nelson called *1001 Ways to Reward Employees*. She realized that to encourage the behaviors, attitudes, and activities that make business development everyone's business, you must constantly recognize employees and show them how much you value them.

Over time, the system was working. In addition to regular performance reviews, all of the managers, including Frank, began to routinely and informally give feedback to employees on the floor. The managers were able to catch employees doing something well and, every now and then, help them with noticeable obstacles. They also came up with "Great Job!" incentives such as recognition in the corporate newsletter and rewards in the form of movie passes and gift certificates, which one of the managers had read, according to research, are two of the most popular employee reward incentives.

Employees, in turn, began to see their value in very real terms. They saw that their contributions mattered and began doing whatever it took to help the company survive the impending technology transition. Following the company-wide meeting, the employees broke into "performance teams" to brainstorm ideas for new products and technology. Utilizing the talents, knowledge, and skills of a cross section of employees from various departments, the teams documented strengths and weaknesses, highlighted skill gaps, and outlined plans to enhance performance. Every performance team communicated results and findings to each other and shared their knowledge. The company posted updates online and encouraged all employees to participate in discussions.

The book, *Raving Fans,* by Ken Blanchard and Sheldon Bowles, shows through the telling of a story, how employees perform great feats of customer service and receive rewards for their efforts. The fictional employees in the story have what they call a "Raving Fan Index" where they measure on a monthly basis for every department every person working at the company. They talk to customers and use internal benchmarks like rework or on-time-delivery scores to put the index together. Everyone who works there knows who his or her customer is, both internal and external. Their Raving Fan Index is tied directly to their own customer base and that counts heavily toward both raises and promotions.

A year later, the company had developed a product that incorporated the new technology. They had even found that along the way, with all employees having been included in decision-making and product development, they

had implemented several new ideas for value-added service. Clients were happy, employees were happy, and
Frank, whose conscience had started the whole thing,
was happy. And, in spite of new business challenges, which
they met with team spirit and togetherness, they worked
happily ever after.

The End

Creating Ways to
Measure BDEB Progress

How many "Franks" do you have in your organization—the kind
of individual who could one day own his or her own company with
your blessing? (Most employees may never want to own their own
company, but they can certainly think and make decisions like owners
at yours). As owners and managers, one of our goals should be to
watch for employees who show initiative and talent in contributing
ideas and leveraging opportunities to proactively represent their
organization to their connections. How many "closers" and
"influencers" exist within each department or division? How could
various BDEB activities be parceled out to individuals who show an
aptitude for making the most of each opportunity? Have you defined what aptitudes are necessary for BDEB activities within your
organization?

Frank's story could be considered an overly optimistic view of the way companies operate. We don't discount that each company brings to BDEB its own set of organizational obstacles and hurdles, and we realize that Frank's company was remarkably free from these things. The point of the story is to simply create an awareness of BDEB by highlighting the process that Frank took to begin to measure and, thereby *value* BDEB activities differently from when he first implemented BDEB.

Think about some of the things your organization must do to develop or enhance your performance evaluation system to include BDEB. To do this, consider this two-step process: First, you must value certain behaviors as part of your business development approach, e.g. community service, continual learning, and sincere helpfulness. Match these behaviors with the specific behaviors that are part of your company's formal job descriptions and who is accountable for them. Second, develop some sample objectives that support these key responsibilities. These objectives will suggest the measures you can use to evaluate performance and pay incentive bonuses. You will then be able to formulate individual development plans. You can do all this systematically by creating your own BDEB Performance Matrix, a tool we strongly recommend that will clarify job expectations and give you greater opportunities for feedback relating to business development responsibilities.

BDEB Performance Matrix

A BDEB Performance Matrix blends attitudes, skills, and knowledge in with your existing employee performance review process. In creating the matrix, you can adapt the roles and responsibilities to specific jobs in your organization. Create your organization's BDEB Performance Matrix by creating a table that answers by each job role the following questions.

- How will BDEB help you do your job?
- What are your individual BDEB activities and roles?
- How will I be measured?
- What will be my reward for being a contributor to BDEB?
- What are my necessary BDEB attitudes, skills, and knowledge?
- What training and development may be necessary for my role-specific BDEB achievement?

By answering all six of these questions for each position/role in your own BDEB Performance Matrix, you will have a better chance of getting the performance you seek. For every individual activity, you need to clarify how it can be measured, how performance can be rewarded, what skills and knowledge are necessary to perform this activity, and what training and development may be necessary.

The BDEB Performance Matrix should incorporate many of the responsibilities that employees already do. In its ideal form, the matrix will simply add these responsibilities in a way that will be seamless additions to employees' jobs. The matrix also shows how in the course of doing their jobs, all positions inter-connect to support a BDEB culture. We've created the matrix based on roles because in a consulting/service-type business, people may have different roles on different projects. The BDEB responsibilities in the following example are tied to roles. Your BDEB Performance Matrix may need to be more position-based. Two important considerations in developing your own matrix are 1) Everyone has jobs and/or roles that are relevant to BDEB responsibilities/accountabilities, and 2) All critical BDEB activities must be assigned to employees who are accountable for them. Below is an example of how we have answered, "What are your individual BDEB roles?" based on these two considerations. We've selected two types of BDEB activities to highlight. You can see a more detailed example of the BDEB Performance Matrix in the Appendix that answers all of the questions.

Activity	What are your individual BDEB roles?			
	GM/VP	**Sales**	**Project Manager**	**Staff**
Account Profiles	I will direct the completion of account profiles for my target prospects and clients in my geographic territory.	I will be responsible for the development and maintenance of my specific account profiles.	I will proactively contribute to the development and maintenance of account profiles.	I will proactively contribute to the development and maintenance of the account profiles.
Channels of Opportunity™	I will direct the collection of data that will become my site's Channels of Opportunity™.	I will document and leverage my site's primary Channels of Opportunity™.	I will make it part of my job to fully understand our primary Channels of Opportunity™.	I will make it part of my job to fully understand our primary Channels of Opportunity™.

For example, if all employees are accountable for contributing to account profiles, but no one in particular is *directing* the effort, account profiles are less likely to be done effectively or on a timely basis. If everyone is accountable for understanding your organization's Channels of Opportunity™, then someone must be accountable for collecting the data and preparing the summary documents.

Once you have created your BDEB Performance Matrix, we recommend that you plan time for evaluating employees. Do you currently have a review process that is done on an annual or quarterly basis? To get better results from BDEB, it is best to increase the frequency of evaluation especially as it relates to business development. After all, if employees are performing the activities that mine the gold, you need to go digging more often for the cache.

Frequent business development evaluation is important for a number of reasons. First, employees will recognize the importance and significance to their work. They will become accustomed to being routinely evaluated regarding their business development activities and will perform at higher standards accordingly. Second, employees will appreciate the regular feedback on their business development performance. This feedback supports positive work behaviors and actions and will go a long way toward establishing a sense of job security and positive customer service behaviors. The third reason is for knowledge management purposes. If employees are being asked to report on their indirect business development activities every three months, for example, managers should be seeing evidence of employees' work in terms of business development leads; gathering employees' ideas for value-added products and services; and having additional opportunities to provide business development coaching/mentoring.

Is Measurement Worth the Effort?

Valuing a variety of business development activities and results improves outcomes. Owners and managers must learn how to measure the softer side against their "hard" business measures by focusing less on the dollars spent and more on the outcomes from those dollars spent.

If you are trying to decide on the level of effort you should put into this element of measurement you can use the following questions as a guide:

- How much more business is out there for my company?
- How much is a qualified prospect worth to us?
- Would our company benefit from increasing our revenue per employee ratio?

Then, compare the cost of buying the publicity and good will that comes as an added value from satisfied customers with the connections you naturally have with employees, suppliers, clients, prospects, and the community.

Measurement doesn't have to be a hard concept but it does take clear definition, diligence, commitment, and consistency. You must learn to value the things that go on in your organization that are silent contributors to business development. There must be a direct link between performance expectations and relevant measures.

Putting Principle 6 Into Action

ACTION Prepare your employees to participate in trade association meetings. Include information about associations in new employee orientation and distribute meeting announcements to staff. Consider rotating employees by department so everyone has a chance to participate. Again, look for those employees who emerge as significant "influencers" for your business at these meetings.

ACTION Create your organization's own "balanced portfolio of business measures" for all areas of your business.

ACTION Develop a customized BDEB Performance Matrix for your organization using the information in this chapter as a guide.

 Evaluate all employees every three or six months with the BDEB Skills Assessment found in Principle 5. The assessment is self-scoring so employees can immediately see their improvement over the last time they took the assessment. The 30 statements are business development ideas for immediate implementation as well.

 As a rule, people do a poor job of documenting their own performance in terms of their daily activities. Encourage employees to record their own observations and reflect on their performance on a weekly basis using their own BDEB Performance Matrix as a tool.

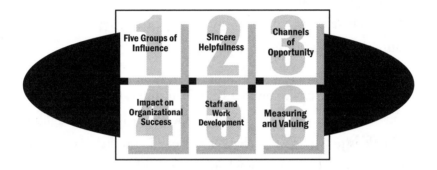

| Five Groups of Influence | Sincere Helpfulness | Channels of Opportunity |
| Impact on Organizational Success | Staff and Work Development | Measuring and Valuing |

Getting to 100%: Building the BDEB Environment

If you've come with us on our walk through the six principles, having stopped to do the exercises (smelling the flowers, so to speak) and meditate on what you've learned, you're probably thinking specifically about your organization and how changing to a BDEB culture can help you meet your business goals. And, if you have read this far, you're probably ready to implement BDEB.

If you've read anything about change (and who hasn't, really?) you know that changing from the old to the new can be pretty hard on people in your organization. Including you. While changing to a

BDEB culture is an exciting time, filled with possibility and opportunity, if not implemented strategically, employees may be intimidated by some of their new responsibilities. William Bridges, in his book, *Managing Transitions*, says that even with "good" change, people will perceive that they have lost something valuable to them. Bridges says "the failure to identify and be ready for the endings and losses that change produces is the largest single problem that organizations in transition encounter."

Rest assured that changing to a BDEB culture can be classified as "good" change, and we've given you specific reasons throughout this book as to why. In this chapter, we're going to help you determine what stands to change when a BDEB philosophy is implemented in your organization. We're also going to show you some specific steps to effectively implement BDEB.

Hopefully by now you've thought of several ways in which you can put many, if not all, of the six BDEB principles to work immediately. Here is one example of a company that is leveraging their internal resources in a way that is natural within the course of their everyday business.

Alcoa Automotive Sheet Facility

Alcoa Automotive Sheet Facility in Danville, Illinois, has an environment that motivates employees to glowingly talk about their company to their individual connections. The employees come to work each day and immediately see a wall entitled "These Are the Reasons We Work Safely." The wall is located near both the cafeteria and time clock and proudly displays photographs of all employees' families. "The whole reason we go to work is to support our family," said Butch Buesing, Maintenance Associate with Alcoa. Buesing and his co-workers appreciate the photographs. They are a source of pride for employees

---

and serve as a reminder as to why their success at work is their families' success at home.

It is obvious to Buesing that Alcoa values family. To encourage more time spent with families, Alcoa has created a work environment with a revolving four 12-hour day work shift where team members get three days off, and no one employee has to work weekends all of the time. (Principle 5) In addition, everyone in the plant knows about every job and its basic description. That way if someone is sick, another qualified person can step in (Principle 2). The employees are also clear about how they impact the organization. Buesing said that his job is to keep the equipment running so Alcoa can meet production and safety goals. (Principle 4)

Alcoa promotes a proactive team environment. In fact, many employees wear t-shirts that boldly say "PROACTIVE" to remind them to think ahead for solutions and ways to better serve customers and fellow co-workers. (Principles 1 & 2) Employees know how the company measures them. All employees receive a quarterly bonus based on three goals—production, delivery, and safety. Employees are also included in a "pay for skills program" where the more you know, the more valuable you are and therefore, the more you are paid. (Principle 6)

It has been said, "positive employee perceptions of work environment are critical to a productive organization." At Alcoa, this rings true. Sales are up, and the company has consistently met their goals in all areas. In shipping, for example, they've met their targets each month. With employee focus now on proactive service and solutions and their knowledge of company goals, the company is actually reaching their goals. And, this measurement is based on when shipments are physically in customers' warehouses. So, not only do they have to be careful about shipping and packaging, they have to guarantee delivery as well.

As in the above example, BDEB is a compelling business model because:

- It helps you leverage the resources that you have, strengthening the things that already make you a successful organization.

- It encourages 100% involvement in helping the organization reach its goals and puts you in a position to develop more business in the most natural and effortless way possible.

- It diminishes finger pointing and departmental segregation and promotes teamwork and collaboration, thereby building employee morale and a spirit for success.

Ken Blanchard says of the seven characteristics of high performing teams, one of the most important characteristics is morale. So, what motivates employees to provide better customer service, seek additional business development opportunities, build stronger relationships, and represent their companies positively and proactively 100% of the time? One of the best ways to motivate employees is to instill in them a strong sense of direction and purpose. Give them meaningful work and show them how their contribution is appreciated and valued. When employees share that indefinable sense of spirit, enthusiasm and pride, they're more than willing to help companies achieve their goals.

Motivation is three parts preparation to one part implementation. In other words, motivating employees can be a lot like programming code—you can spend hundreds of hours developing code so that a simple 30-second transaction functions flawlessly. The key to motivating employees is that it takes a lot more planning what you're going to do and what's appropriate to do than actually doing it.

Motivation is also an internal force. The fact is, other people can't actually motivate us—we must motivate ourselves. Inspiration, on the other hand, is external. We can inspire others. As managers, it is our responsibility to **inspire** our employees to meet higher performance expectations. We can inspire in many ways.

We inspire by modeling.

If you are a parent, you know that a large part of parenting is modeling the types of behaviors and attitudes that we want to see in our children. For example, if, as you tell your child not to talk with food in his mouth. . .your mouth is full of food. . .you probably aren't modeling properly! It's no different at work, and it's even more important. If you want to encourage an environment of sincere helpfulness, for example, be helpful. Let employees see that you are willing to help make copies for an important client deliverable if its deadline is approaching and help is needed.

We inspire by being effective leaders.

Leadership is a silent skill. It's not about saying you're the leader but by demonstrating effective leadership qualities such as routinely providing information and feedback, trusting and empowering employees, communicating expectations, and demonstrating genuine interest in employees' work. Leadership is about having a passion for the organization's vision of the future and having the courage to share that vision.

We inspire by providing our employees with work that is enriching, by giving them responsibilities, and holding them accountable.

Consider the employee who is given an extra challenge because her manager believes she is the best person for the job. Think how good that employee must feel knowing that she's got her manager's trust and respect. Know how inspired she must be to do the best job she can and then be recognized for her accomplishment.

We inspire by finding out what makes our employees tick and then winding them up a notch.

Use the ASK WHY Model™ in Principle 5, and you'll be able to find out what motivates simply by asking questions and listening with genuine interest to the answers.

We inspire by appreciating our employees.

Say "thank you" for their contributions often. Recognize their efforts privately and publicly. Tell them, simply, "I appreciate you."

If you create a motivating environment for employees, the result will be a work environment where both you and employees can do your best work. And, it should seem fairly obvious that doing your best work elevates self esteem which perpetuates and *motivates* high performing work behaviors. You see, it's one of those cycles where one feeds the other and the more you sow, the more you reap.

Eight Implementation Steps

There are eight important steps that are necessary for implementing a BDEB culture within any organization. Each step is systematic and should be performed in the order listed.

S
T
E
P

Recognize an opportunity for improved business development.
While traveling to present BDEB to a group of managers for a large business consulting firm, we had the good fortune to visit on the airplane with an investment banker specializing in mergers and acquisitions. During our conversation, which gravitated to the topic of BDEB, the investment banker said that the single most important thing to an equity partner is one word: growth.

In earlier chapters, we've talked about the many reasons why you might recognize an opportunity for improved business development in your organization. Here are a few:

- You want to grow.
- You want to increase profit margins.

- You want to gain a competitive edge in the marketplace.
- You want to attract and retain qualified and "attitudinally" fit employees.
- You want a low cost way to beef up your marketing and advertising.

You must realize why BDEB is right for you and then set goals that help you get where you want to be. Renaissance Government Solutions (RGS), having embraced BDEB as their corporate philosophy, realized that to become the company they want to grow into, they had to first examine how they were developing business in the first place. "Business development has been kind of a hobby to the 75% of our organization not titled sales and marketing," said Tom DiMartino, RGS president. "BDEB is a cultural shift for our organization." The graphic below illustrates how RGS plans to get to 100% employee involvement in business development activities.

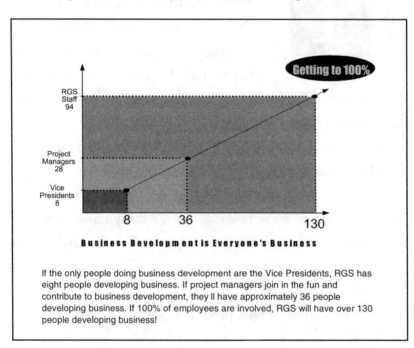

Business Development is Everyone's Business

If the only people doing business development are the Vice Presidents, RGS has eight people developing business. If project managers join in the fun and contribute to business development, they'll have approximately 36 people developing business. If 100% of employees are involved, RGS will have over 130 people developing business!

The first thing you need to do is decide why BDEB is right for your organization. What is your overall goal for implementing BDEB? Would you like to see more business coming in the door? If that's the case, what if employees perceive that you already have enough business since they are too busy to get their existing work done now? People aren't in the market for solutions to problems they don't see, acknowledge, and understand. That's why you must communicate to employees what your specific goals are, such as getting more *profitable* business and bringing in enough business to justify adding staff. It may be useful to open your books to show them how hard they work simply to pay the bills. Educate them on cash flow and how it affects your ability to make important decisions for your organization. Create their support by talking openly and honestly and soliciting their help and ideas.

Do you wish to implement BDEB because you want to improve employee morale and job satisfaction? Be warned that implementing BDEB the wrong way could produce opposite results. BDEB will be a significant change for many organizations, and the wise Mark Twain once said that the only person who likes change is a wet baby! Change, in general, has a funny way of intimidating many who believe that a different way means less for them in the long run. People process change by saying things like: "Am I going to lose my job? Am I going to be able to do the things that they are asking me to do?" The fear of failure and the unknown are innate feelings that often accompany change in the workplace. The "what's in it for me" way of thinking plays a strong part any time you launch a new initiative, or in the case of BDEB, a new philosophy for doing business.

Politicians know how hard it is to encourage people to change their minds about something. Michael McDaniel, Chairman of the Indiana Republican State Committee, says, "The toughest thing to do is persuade . . . because you're asking someone to do something that they didn't intend to do." Political strategists know that you must first know the audience to whom you're communicating and then tailor your message to them. Push their hot buttons. Talk *to* them, not *at* them. To implement the BDEB principles within your organization, show employees the benefits of BDEB to both the organization and ultimately to them. With a bonus plan in place, you're well on your way to demonstrating your commitment for their support.

Assess your organization's strategic strengths for BDEB.

Before any customization can begin, you must gather very specific information about your organization. You must document your organization's strengths and weaknesses regarding business development and the activities all employees can do to increase sales. Research several key areas of your business including market factors and industry trends, organizational structure, management support, and marketing and communications. This includes the Channels of Opportunity™ exercise found in Principle 3.

Draft a summary of your findings and use this information as you move forward with BDEB. Factor in the number of employees you have and the type of products you sell. For example, if your company sells consumer products such as potato chips, your BDEB opportunities are higher since all five of your groups of influence are comprised of your potential customers. This is where you make the decision as to how appropriate BDEB is for your organization. Armed with specific information about your organization, you are ready to begin developing a customized BDEB implementation plan.

The Importance of Management Support

Managers are the key to keeping employees focused on organizational goals and getting all employees involved. Without management support, many programs would die on the vine before having had the chance to blossom and produce fruit. It's no different for implementing a cultural philosophy such as BDEB.

Prior to any implementation of BDEB, you must be confident that you have all managers on board because, without management support, BDEB will become a "flavor of the month," and subsequently lose its taste only to wash away into oblivion. Explore your current level of management support for valuing and supporting BDEB principles. Do managers communicate organizational goals (mission, vision, values, profits, etc.)? Do they know your organization's top three Channels of Opportunity™, and do they share this information with employees often? Do managers know the status of customer satisfaction in your organization? Do they effectively communicate performance expectations to their staff? Do they routinely provide performance feedback to their staff? Do they understand how each job role in the organization contributes to business development? (The BDEB Performance Matrix will help them with this last point.)

If you answer "no" to any of these questions, you've got some work to do—work that could be included as part of your BDEB implementation plan. Get managers enthused about BDEB by providing them with whatever information is necessary to help them see BDEB's value. The goal is to enlist the support of all managers in the creation of your customized BDEB implementation plan.

Customize your BDEB implementation plan.

Implementing a BDEB culture will be different for each company. What works for one company will probably not work for another company in a different industry. That's why the information you gather in Step 2 is so critical to the success of customizing your own plan. You will be creating BDEB tools specific to your organization's needs and setting measurement standards. You'll be working with managers to create a strong foundation of support for rollout to the rest of the employees. And, you'll be uncovering specific concerns among the employees about BDEB—possible negative perceptions they have about what they will be doing in the new work culture.

Change is all in the perception of what is happening to the individual. Martha Grayson, consultant for Corporate Health Promotion at St. Vincent Hospitals & Health Services, says that 70% of all healthcare office visits are related to the stress of change, prompting the healthcare industry to conduct extensive research on stress in the workplace. Grayson says that it is important to acknowledge employee stress during times of change in order to manage it. Stress will occur as a result of implementing BDEB. After all, it is a change and as William Bridges says nothing undermines organizational change as much as the failure to think through who will have to let go of what when change occurs.

What do employees stand to lose with BDEB? For those employees who have always worked in functions not related to client interaction, a loss of comfort and control could occur when presented with BDEB. People leave their comfort zones when they step out into the world and actually begin networking with others at association meetings and events. Just the thought of saying the information bite is enough to make some people break out into a nervous sweat. Managers will lose control for a while as well. They will feel like their workload has increased because of the extra information coming in and because of their responsibility to measure results.

Identify some ways in which your employees currently make BDEB work in your organization by revisiting the BDEB Self Assessment in Principle 5. The assessment will also help you identify what behaviors and attitudes need to be modified.

Customizing Roles and Responsibilities

You will be creating your own BDEB Performance Matrix during Step 3 of the implementation process. We discussed the Performance Matrix at length in Principle 6. Refer to the sample performance matrix in the Appendix and customize your own using the questions as a guide.

Once you have properly defined each job role within your organization and how employees can naturally contribute to business development, you are well on your way to customizing your implementation plan. The Performance Matrix will define BDEB behaviors and activities, giving employees a strong sense of direction and purpose. Once you share the BDEB Performance Matrix with them, you'll find that many of their initial fears regarding a BDEB cultural change will go away. The matrix will show them that if they aren't in a sales position with their company, for example, they will not be expected to make any prospecting calls for new business. They will be able to see the natural connections between themselves and others in the organization.

If employees think that they're too busy to add BDEB responsibilities to their jobs, remove this obstacle by first acknowledging it openly. Assure them that BDEB could be adding to their jobs. But you can demonstrate that most of the items on the BDEB "to do" list are activities that are already in some way embedded in employees' existing work. You can do this by having employees acknowledge the things that they already do that are listed on the matrix. Ask them to brainstorm extra ways they could reasonably contribute to business development.

Customizing Rewards and Incentives

Once you have educated employees on their BDEB roles, you should encourage positive attitudes, skills, and behaviors by recognizing and rewarding them. What do employees get if they become a part of 100% business development involvement? Tom DiMartino, when asked what the benefit to RGS employees will be if they contribute to business development said, "It's not what's going to happen to you if you don't do BDEB. It's what's going to happen to you if you *do*." This is where rewards and incentives come in.

You'll be creating systems for recognizing and rewarding positive and productive BDEB behavior. Incentives stimulate people to action by appealing to self-interest. Put simply, they "mean anything that helps employees boost a company's bottom line." Incentives can vary from company to company and employee to employee. Which ones work for you depends on your corporate culture and the state at which you are ready to change to a BDEB environment.

Many owners think of monetary incentives first, such as profit-sharing plans, company bonuses, and cash rewards, as the things that employees need for a performance boost. Those incentives are nice benefits for the powerful contributions employees will be giving. After all, when they embrace the philosophy that business development is their business, employees will be doing things that will contribute to the proposals, lead generation, and customer service.

We prefer to see financial incentives as simply funds, based on the overall success of the organization, that are shared by all employees. There are other kinds of incentives that can be used to build employee confidence and increase recognition for a job well done. Promotions and advancements, special assignments, raises based on performance evaluation, job stability, and recognition in corporate-wide communications promotes loyalty, better customer service, and gives employees a sense that they are appreciated.

Look at Walt Disney World, which has over 180 recognition programs, and is constantly looking for additional ways to reward employees. And, consider the employee benefits program that Ford Motor Company recently initiated. They gave 350,000 employees a computer, printer, and home Internet service for $5 a month. Ford believes this investment in technology for their people will enhance productivity while working to retain qualified workers within their workforce.

A 1999 survey studying employee commitment by Walker Information cites that "only three in ten employees feel an obligation to stay with their current employer." Information like this certainly points to the benefits of creating recognition and incentive strategies for retaining employees. More importantly, these strategies should be focused on rewarding BDEB performance to perpetuate the behaviors that will help your company thrive. Check out these web sites for more ideas about employee incentives: www.Incentivemarketing.org; www.Recognition.org; and www.Workforce.com.

The key to providing BDEB performance incentives is to understand in detail the activities you value. (Again, the Channels of Opportunity™ exercise in Principle 3 will serve as your blueprint for determining your most productive channels and activities of value to your organization). Then, connect the activities you value with incentives you know your employees value, and you've got a winning combination of incentives that will promote continued BDEB behavior.

Customizing Your Communications Plan

Consider laying a positive foundation from the beginning. First, let people know you're reading a book about business development. In fact, consider having others in your organization read the book. Later, you can all discuss the ideas and determine which ones are most relevant to your situation. Then, plan for and begin to implement your BDEB communications campaign. In times of corporate transition, it is important to have a well-planned communications strategy in place to educate employees on each step along the way. Involve as many employees as possible in the information gathering called out in Step 2.

Often, a change effort includes some kind of training intervention. Implementing a communications strategy along with the training informs employees in a consistent manner and helps to prevent questions about non-technical issues during training. Examples of activities that can be included within a communications strategy are newsletters, job aids, "lunch and learns," contests, and promotional items such as key chains, magnets, mouse pads, "nerf" balls, ink pens, and coffee cups.

Here are specific suggestions for planning and implementing a BDEB communications strategy in your organization:

- Organize a communications committee to develop and implement each strategy and to do any reporting and writing.
- Set a routine communications schedule so employees know when to expect information.
- Always seek feedback from those receiving the information. This feedback will continue to steer the message in the direction needed to properly dispatch information and news.
- When in doubt, ask. Go to the source and ask employees what it will take to lessen the effect of change. Ask them to suggest low cost methods of getting the information out.
- Always do what you say you will do. For example, if employees

learn in your communications that the training will involve follow-up coaching sessions, provide follow-up coaching sessions. If for some reason, these sessions are no longer planned or needed, tell employees the reason for the change.

- If you mail paychecks or stubs to staff, use this as an opportunity to communicate BDEB principles.

- Create a section in the corporate newsletter for a business development corner with information about the three key areas of business development: Presenting Self, Knowledge of the Company, and Proactive Business Development.

- Publish a formal information bite about the company and let employees know that they can substitute their own words to share this information with others as long as they hit specific anchors.

Employees perceive any change as certain doom when rumblings go uncontrolled. A well-planned communications strategy when blended with the other BDEB implementation steps will:

- Surface employees' concerns, questions, and ideas and encourage them to communicate
- Support employees with information and ideas to encourage awareness and acceptance
- Enhance general skills that contribute to BDEB success
- Inspire confidence and competence
- Alleviate fear of change and frustration
- Improve transfer of learning with practical ideas and advice

STEP 4

Enhance your work environment to support BDEB.

It is a common practice for companies to provide anyone with direct sales and marketing responsibilities with a practical business environment in which to work. We recommend that you develop and nurture a work environment that supports business development for all employees. This is especially important for all employees who work directly with your customers, such as project consultants and managers, customer service representatives, and equipment technicians. These employees are your single most strategically-placed business development ambassadors, and they can only support BDEB when they have the proper tools and work environment.

Creating a Productive BDEB Work Environment

If your organization is one where managers and consultants maintain offices at the client site, consider the dilemma of one IT consulting firm. Their business development managers doubled as project managers. While working with clients, they were expected to develop additional business for their company. In fact, their performance was measured by how much new business they brought in the door. It is extremely difficult to conduct meaningful business development activities and remain professional while housed *exclusively* at a client location. Relocating these employees somewhere other than the client's office does not have to be a huge investment. After all, it would give them private space for important phone calls and walls for posting positive reminders and goal statements.

Consider what type of work environment is necessary for all employees to contribute to business development. Observe the activities and work environment considerations typically provided to sales and marketing professionals and include as many of them as possible in your BDEB culture.

Uncovering Your Organization's Disincentives

Disincentives are situations that exist in the organization that may have a negative impact on getting to 100%. Disincentives are very common and must be dealt with swiftly. As you've read this book, have you become aware of any disincentives that may be built into your systems and work cultures? Here are common examples of disincentives:

- Your marketing materials tout your organization's skills and abilities in a certain area, when in fact your staff does not possess these strengths.
- You measure performance of your employees by volume while you say you value quality.
- You want your inbound phone lines answered by the third ring but the call volume is too high for one receptionist.
- Answering calls and greeting guests should be your receptionist's first priority, but she is held accountable for getting important paperwork done for others in the office.
- You want sales clerks to help customers on the floor immediately, but when the phone rings, they are expected to answer it.

- You want employees to work as a team, yet your reward system is based on individual performance.
- You've made such a big deal about the contributions of your sales team, you've managed to devalue the contributions of your other departments.
- You encourage all employees to bring in leads but your follow-through on these leads is weak.

After implementation of BDEB, you can uncover your own disincentives by talking with employees and asking, "What problems are you having with BDEB and how can we solve them?" By that time, they will have had a chance to absorb the tasks listed on their BDEB Performance Matrix and should have a clearer idea of the things they need in order to meet BDEB expectations.

You should be aware that while incorporating BDEB into your organizational culture, you or others in your organization will be gathering data and assessing your current situation. As a result, you will probably discover some of your organization's "blemishes." This is good because it presents you with an opportunity to minimize the disincentives prior to the implementation of BDEB. However, try not to get sidetracked into trying to change other things about your culture that do not need changing to be able to implement BDEB immediately. As John Wooden stated so eloquently, "Do not let what you cannot do interfere with what you can do." We believe that most organizations can implement components of BDEB immediately by looking at and leveraging existing strengths. What are your organization's strengths to help you get started?

Business Development and Knowledge Management

Once you've implemented the BDEB Skills Assessment, done your discovery using the ASK WHY Model™, analyzed the data, and found your organization's performance gaps, you are ready to begin slowly implementing BDEB into your work culture. Along with the BDEB activity comes information in the form of business development leads, intellectual capital, and reports. How will you manage all of this knowledge? Are you fully prepared to read all of the reports that could potentially be generated? For example, if everything stops at a senior manager's desk, how will others benefit from the collection of data? The true essence of knowledge management requires reasonable forms of data repository and retrieval options. To benefit fully, this corporate memory should be available on a just-in-time (J.I.T.) basis.

Consider developing a reporting structure for business development activities. One of the best ways to manage corporate memory relating to clients is with an account profile. An account profile is a format for the collection of information regarding each client contact, its organization, and the project and/or opportunity. It is a tool that will help manage business development activities and opportunities as well.

Account profiles can become a significant asset to the organization for the following reasons:
- They can be used to assess market potential during planning sessions.
- They can be used to quickly acclimate new employees to a particular geographic market.

- They can be used to plan proactive business development efforts.

- They can give your organization a deeper understanding of your clients and their organizational issues so you can provide support at a much higher level. As a result, you will uncover many more opportunities to be of service and will, therefore, become more referable.

- With more information about your clients and prospects, you can manage your territory better.

- As you become more experienced at this information gathering process, you will become more strategic about it as well.

Account profiles can be initiated at a local level as a manager or sales person collects information on all of the prospects in the geographic territory. Project managers and customer service representatives may also develop and/or add to profiles. For example, a project manager may uncover a potential opportunity for an add-on project. By adding this information to the account profiles, the person with the responsibility for developing that potential will be alerted to the opportunity and its degree of business development readiness. The bottom line is that everyone in the organization should be accountable in some way for the proactive and continuous contributions to account profiles.

We recommend that all information be collected and stored on an electronic knowledge repository that allows you to indefinitely enhance information. Very similar to web technology, an ideal account profiling system should allow you to access specific data by clicking on abbreviated data and immediately linking to a separate page that has more detailed information. For example, a person visiting the profile might click on the "Contact" field and learn how long that person has been with the agency, his/her education and work experience background, special interests, and other personal information.

Enhance employee BDEB competency.

When employees have been doing their jobs for a while, they probably feel in control and competent. Implementing BDEB into your organizational culture could result in a brief period when employees go back to that first day on the job. They will feel unsure and may experience an identity crisis as a result of BDEB. But, the Chinese word for "crisis" is a combination of two characters: danger and opportunity. Rather than becoming so intimidated by the danger during this crisis that they miss the opportunity, it will be your job to help employees enhance their BDEB competencies and therefore, look for opportunities to develop business in the natural course of their jobs.

You should be exploring employee needs as they relate to BDEB and conducting what the training industry calls a "gap analysis." A gap analysis simply follows a performance-based training approach which prompts us to first determine what specific skills or behaviors we want to see more or less of in our employees. It helps us identify our current performance gaps. Then, it helps us clarify what specific impact closing these gaps will have on our business. Put simply:

· Where are you now?

- Where do you want to be?
- What do you have to do to get there?

This information will tell you where you must train employees for appropriate BDEB attitudes, skills, and knowledge. Any training and development approach should be designed to help employees perform better on the job. And, for employees to be successful within their organization, it is important that their performance be in line with the organization's goals. Training that is not aligned with the organization's goals will cause employee cynicism, resulting in a lack of commitment on their part.

Performance can be classified in three levels of proficiency: Awareness, Competence, and Mentor. Implementing BDEB within your organization should factor in each level when considering evaluation and measurement.

- An awareness level will give employees a general understanding of the business development concepts and activities and an awareness of how these concepts relate to their own individual work situations.
- A competence level will ensure that employees have a complete understanding of all practical business development concepts and activities. Specific competence includes: knowing products and services and client business needs, primary channels of opportunity, and their impact on organizational success; giving feedback; seeking opportunities to provide value-added service to clients; and conducting basic client communications. Testing is recommended at this level.

· A mentor level will allow employees to teach business development concepts to others. Employees will be able to provide business development coaching and idea generation for new business development activities.

One question to ask during performance appraisals and job interviews for new employees is, does the person have proper BDEB attitudes? For example, do they show evidence of having pleasantly served customers, sincerely helped co-workers and business contacts, and openly sought more information in order to do their jobs better? Southwest Airlines has a unique approach to the interview process by avoiding stock interview questions about work experience and focusing more on questions related to candidates' sense of compassion, humor, and service. Consider asking questions regarding the person's past record of service specifically to the Five Groups of Influence™.

Test site BDEB rollout.

**S
T
E
P** **6**

If you are a company with branch offices throughout different parts of the country, we recommend that you roll out BDEB to one site first and use your observations to further tweak your implementation plans. Ideally, it would be better to implement BDEB at the site where you are located so you can remain at the pulse of activity and be readily accessible for any questions.

When you officially roll out BDEB, you will be monitoring employee accountability for the BDEB principles. Using the BDEB

Performance Matrix, employees will begin to do parts of their jobs differently, and they will be finding ways to improve their current systems to support their continued BDEB involvement. Step 6 will also involve a hearty exchange of feedback between managers and employees looking for answers to that earlier question, "What problems are you having with BDEB?" You will be able to get the bugs out of the process and will have time to prepare a "Most Frequently Asked Questions" document for other corporate offices.

Organization-wide BDEB rollout.

When rolling BDEB out to the entire organization, you will formally begin the process of holding employees accountable for BDEB activities and measuring their results. As a rule, people do not want to be held accountable for things they don't have control over. That's why it's important to let employees discuss factors affecting their performance and determine what they do and don't have control over. In fact, both employees and managers show a resistance to the whole concept of measurement. Managers who think they are too busy to begin measuring should reconsider. The use of measurement should become an integrated component of their job as managers of people and processes. If formal measurement points to a deficiency in the manager's ability, let managers know that support will be available.

Employees who are uncomfortable with the unknown should experience relief when management routinely shares measurement results. One idea would be for employees to get together and share with each other the opportunities they've had within the last period to connect with the important Channels of Opportunity™, use the information bite, and be sincerely helpful.

People need to know how they fit in. As managers, it is our responsibility to help employees understand their impact and to help them continue to develop into the best they can be. BDEB can be fun because there are many intrinsic rewards for building rapport and relationships with others.

Celebrate BDEB success.

Celebrate BDEB success, no matter how small! Celebrate after each step of the implementation process has been completed, and create a ceremony for the beginning of new steps. It takes a lot of hard work to change a process or culture and all stakeholders should be rewarded for their efforts and successes. No effort should go without celebration. Consider rewarding them as a group because the entire company is going to do better with BDEB.

And, resist the urge to use measurement to micro manage or control people! Your mother wasn't trying to control your growth when she made a tick mark on your bedroom door jamb each month—she was simply helping you celebrate how big you were getting! Measurement is another tool for supporting BDEB performance and should be viewed as a way to celebrate success and improve situations in a non-threatening way.

Finally, recognize the results that come from BDEB behaviors and activities. Publicly praise individuals in staff meetings or in the company newsletter; give dinner certificates or movie passes for two; personally recognize individuals with handwritten notes of thanks; or even dedicate a reserved parking spot recognizing an individual who made a significant contribution to business development for any given month.

Ending on the idea of celebration is fitting. Once you have successfully implemented BDEB into your culture, you'll have reasons to celebrate! Envision your new corporate culture where 100% of your employees are involved in helping the company reach its goals. Envision 100% of your employees leveraging their connections, both personally and professionally, to promote your company. Envision, if you will, business development has become everyone's business in your organization. As a result, profitable business is yours, and employees are happy to recommend your company to their friends as *the* place in town to work.

Celebrate the fact that BDEB will quickly become as second nature to managers and employees as many of the things that they already do. They will begin to recognize these activities for what they are— valuable business development activities that can bring your organization greater success in meeting the business challenges of tomorrow.

Epilogue

It has been said that if you are not moving forward, then you are moving backward. This is not the direction that most organizations have in mind when they hang out that proverbial shingle! Once we become conscious of this fundamental truth, most of us typically choose to move forward. This forward movement is a form of renewal, and in the business world, renewal usually falls into two primary categories: 1) Research and development and 2) Business development. Research and development is the development of new and improved products and services. Business development is the development of new and expanded client relationships. When you recognize the benefits of renewal, you realize it is the lifeblood of the organization. This book deals with business development as renewal.

As we hope we've convinced you, business development isn't just the job of the sales and marketing department. Contributions to an

217

organization's business development effort come from all job positions --receptionists, line managers, customer service representatives, accounts receivable clerks, engineers, and maintenance engineers. In this book, we have tried to encourage employee ownership in the organization's products and goals, which will help break down the barriers and negative stereotypes of the job of "sales." Your work culture can shift to that of *everyone* "doing their part" for business development, resulting in more sales and higher profits!

The ideas and principles within this book will help you maximize your marketing budgets. Get everyone on the payroll helping to promote the company. Multiply sales without adding to sales staff. And make your biggest monthly investment (payroll) work twice as hard. By creating an environment that promotes greater job satisfaction, you will ultimately reduce employee turnover and improve your capacity to recruit the talent you need to grow your business.

We dedicate this book to the hardworking business owners and managers of small businesses. We suspect you have been carrying too much of the business development load and deserve some relief. We are working from the assumption that you are reading this book to learn new ways to increase profits, improve employee morale, or inspire opportunities for additional public relations. You may have been successful thus far in your business and are simply looking for a way to get more of that success. We applaud you for seeking BDEB as one initiative that will improve your organization.

On the other hand, you may have read this book and realized that you and your managers are already doing a lot of the things that we say are critical for a true BDEB environment. Since we chose to write this book directed to owners and managers who aren't yet practicing BDEB activities, we hope that you aren't offended with its tone, but rather re-energized in your business development efforts. Hopefully, you picked up additional ideas to help you on your journey. (We'd love to hear from you regarding any success stories you have had relative to BDEB!)

This book is not an all-or-nothing proposition. Most of the action ideas found within these pages, if implemented individually, can have an immediate and positive effect on your business and its bottom line. Taken as a whole, this book can help you get exponential results. However, this is not a 90-day program. Putting all six principles in place at the same time would be an overwhelming task—a task that no one person can do. It takes the involvement of a team of committed individuals who are working to achieve 100% employee BDEB involvement.

Throughout the six principles, we encourage you to delegate as much as possible of the work identified in each principle's action items. In certain instances, we gave you instructions on how to facilitate a discussion or how to divide the work into manageable pieces. (How do you eat an elephant? One bite at a time!) Remember that we want you to actually do the things we are recommending so you can get the results we talk about in the book.

Each principle within this book links with the others, and all of the principles link with the concept of connections to the Five Groups of Influence™. Our goal in writing this book, however, was to make each chapter stand alone in its information about the principle. Everyone is busy, and unfortunately many of us do not have the luxury to sit down and read a book from cover to cover. Each principle will give you several ideas for you to begin plans to customize and implement BDEB quickly within your organization.

We believe that there is a fine line between what you have heard throughout your life, what you know intrinsically, and what you have read somewhere. Naturally, as we age, we collect wisdom and ideas much like a snowball grows in size as it rolls toward its destination. We have pulled together a variety of resources to position the BDEB philosophy and hope you appreciate the collection of data and stories within this book. In addition, there are many good books on the subjects of marketing and selling your services. If you determine that you need to step up your formal sales and marketing efforts, you will find some recommended reading identified in the Appendix.

And, finally, thank you for buying this book! We hope you'll appreciate your investment and refer *Business Development is Everyone's Business* to others within your Five Groups of Influence™.

End Notes

First Chapter
Transforming Corporate Culture, David Drennan
Liberation Management, Tom Peters

Principle 1
Word-of-Mouth Marketing, Jerry Wilson
Raving Fans, Ken Blanchard and Sheldon Bowles
James McEachern, Chairman of the Board and CEO of Tom James Company as told to Robert Shook in *The Greatest Sales Stories Ever Told: From the World's Best Salespeople.*

Principle 2
"Training with Quality," by Ted Cocheu, *Training & Development*, May 1992
How to Win Friends and Influence People, Dale Carnegie
Rain Making, Ford Harding
Selling for Dummies, Tom Hopkins

Principle 3
Word-of-Mouth Marketing, Jerry Wilson

Principle 4
Reengineering the Corporation, Michael Hammer
"No. 1 Company Secrets: Share it all with employees, soup to nuts," *Inc. Tech*, 1999
The Happiest Workers in the World, The Inc./Gallup Survey, May 21, 1996.

"301 Great Management Ideas from America's Most Innovative Small Companies," Edited by Leslie Brokaw, *Inc.* Magazine.

Principle 5
Competitive Advantage Through People, Jeffrey Pfeffer
Reinventing Work: Professional Service Firm 50, Tom Peters
"Career Insurance for Today's World," by Derwin Fox, *Training & Development,* March 1996 (Odetics).

Principle 6
Robert Shook, *The Greatest Sales Stories Ever Told: From The World's Best Salespeople*
How to Master the Art of Selling, Tom Hopkins
The Tipping Point, Malcolm Gladwell
The Talent Solution, Edward L. Gubman
"The Human Side of a Technology Launch," *Training & Development,* February 1997
101 Great Management Ideas, Bob Nelson
Raving Fans, Ken Blanchard and Sheldon Bowles

Getting to 100%: Implementing BDEB
Managing Transitions, William Bridges
Rebecca Ganzel, "You Want Fries with That Presentation?" July 1999, *Presentations*
"Keeping Spirits up when Times are Down" Shari Caudron, *Personnel Journal,* August 1996 (Ford Motor Company.)
1999 Employee Relationship Report Benchmark, Walker Information and Hudson Institute, Indianapolis, Indiana
"Overcoming Mind Traps: Self-change and its implications for the HRD Professional" Tom Rusk, *The 1990 Annual: Developing Human Resources.*

Appendix

Creating an Information Bite

Channels of Opportunity Level One

Channels of Opportunity Level Two

BDEB Skills Assessment

Sample BDEB Performance Matrix

Sample Opportunity Focused Account Profile

Recommended Reading

About the Authors

Creating an Information Bite

1. What is the name of your organization?

2. What does the organization do?

3. How many years has the organization been in business?

4. How many employees does it have?

5. Does the organization have a unique niche or product line?

6. What kinds of products or services does it sell?

7. What are the organization's customers?

8. What does customer service mean to the organization?

9. How does the organization currently support sales or business development?

Who Do You Work For and
What Does Your Company Do?
(Write your BRIEF answer in the space below.)

Channels of Opportunity

Level One			
Client Name	Project	Proposal/Project Amount	Won/ Lost

Channels of Opportunity

Level Two			
Generation 1	Generation 2	Generation 3	Generation 4

BDEB Skills Assessment

Instructions: The following self-assessment relates to how you contribute to business development in your organization. Please write the number that most applies to you next to the statements below. If you write in 3, for example, you believe that you do that activity most of the time. Add up your scores and transfer them to the Assessing My Score section.

4 - All of the time   **3 - Most of the time**   **2 - Some of the time**   **1 - None of the time**

1. _____I say thank you.

2. _____I have gotten to know the organization inside and out.

3. _____I keep my work space clean and neat.

4. _____I dress professionally and appropriately in the event a client visits our office.

5. _____I ask questions.

6. _____I ask for business cards and hand them out often.

7. _____I am not afraid to say, "I don't know, but I can get that information for you."

8. _____I obtain company literature showcasing products and services.

9. _____I know who my company's clients are and what they do.

10. _____I smile a lot, face to face and over the phone.

11. _____I ask to be included in decisions, optional projects, and new product launches.

12. _____I set aside time for making contacts that focus on customer satisfaction.

13. _____I share my ideas with others.

14. _____I am aware of who is making decisions, and get to know what they think.

15. _____I participate in groups in my company to brainstorm best business development practices.

16. _____I say "I'm sorry" when needed.

17. _____If I state a problem, I present a possible solution.

18. _____I am a mentor/coach.

4 - All of the time **3 - Most of the time** **2 - Some of the time** **1 - None of the time**

19. ____I believe in taking personal responsibility for my actions.

20. ____I have a complete list of all employees within my company and their phone numbers.

21. ____I participate in volunteerism in the community.

22. ____ I document my successes so that I may support my professional advancement.

23. ____I ask for frequent and timely feedback.

24. ____I treat my co-workers like they are my customers.

25. ____When planning my daily to do items, I plan time for interruptions.

26. ____I try to follow up when I have brought in a business lead.

27. ____I seek out opportunities to share what I do with others.

28. ____I return all phone calls promptly.

29. ____ I try to get the information to do my job well.

30. ____I send thank you cards and articles to contacts when appropriate.

Assessing Your Score

Presenting Yourself	Understanding Your Organization	Proactive Business Development
1.____	2. ____	3. ____
4.____	5. ____	6. ____
7.____	8. ____	9. ____
10.____	11.____	12.____
13.____	14.____	15.____
16.____	17.____	18.____
19.____	20.____	21.____
22.____	23.____	24.____
25.____	26.____	27.____
28.____	29.____	30.____

Totals _____   _____   _____

40 - 32   Great   You are contributing to business development!

31 - 22   Good   You are doing most of the things it takes to be a contributor in the business development effort.

21 - Below   Needs Improvement   Look for ways to get help in this area. You can start with the ideas on this list.

Sample BDEB Performance Matrix

Activity	How will BDEB contribute to both your company and your own success?			
	GM/VP	Sales	Project Manager	Staff
Account Profiles		I will have BDEB Tools, e.g., account profiles, which will provide me with better information to be able to target our key prospects.	I will have access to a place to quickly report information as I become aware of it regarding clients, the potential for new business add-ons, and client referrals.	
Channels of Opportunity ™	My Channels of Opportunity™ will highlight best opportunities for new business growth and will direct me more efficiently toward getting more business.	My Channels of Opportunity™ will highlight best opportunities for new business growth and will direct me more efficiently toward getting more business.	I will have an awareness of our specific Channels of Opportunity™ and will know how I can contribute to enhanced profits in these channels.	I will have an awareness of our specific Channels of Opportunity™ and will know how I can contribute to enhanced profits in these channels.
100% Positive and Proactive Business Development	I will no longer be solely responsible for seeking and developing new business opportunities because business development responsibilities will be shared with 100% of employees.	I will have 100% BDEB support from all employees, which will enhance my ability to close more business.	I will be able to, with my knowledge of all that my company has to offer and specific area of expertise, solidify our company's standing as vendor of choice.	I will know and understand the core services and will be able to answer questions about our company. I will know who to direct people to for answers to which I do not have immediate access. I will have on-going opportunities to contribute to customer satisfaction, product development, and service delivery excellence. I will know how my role impacts the bottom line. I will know, as will others in the organization, where my skills and knowledge can best be utilized on projects.
	[Plus everything listed in "staff" category.]	[Plus everything listed in "staff" category.]	[Plus everything listed in "staff" category.]	

229

Activity	What are your individual BDEB roles?			
	GM/VP	Sales	Project Manager	Staff
Account Profiles	I will direct the completion of account profiles for my target prospects and clients in my geographic territory.	I will be responsible for the development and maintenance of my specific account profiles.	I will proactively contribute to the development and maintenance of account profiles.	I will proactively contribute to the development and maintenance of the account profiles.
Channels of Opportunity ™	I will direct the collection of data that will become my site's Channels of Opportunity™. I will oversee the usage of this data to maximize business development opportunities.	I will document and leverage my site's primary Channels of Opportunity™. I will collaborate with Project Managers and staff for maximizing business development opportunities.	I will make it part of my job to fully understand our primary Channels of Opportunity™.	I will make it part of my job to fully understand our primary Channels of Opportunity™. I will positively and proactively represent the company to everyone with whom I come in contact including my connections with suppliers, clients, prospects, employees, and the community.
Communications	I will include all employees in routine communications regarding BDEB progress, successes, and opportunities.	I will provide routine communications on BDEB progress, success, and opportunities.	I will provide BDEB feedback to all direct reports and support them in their personal development plans. I will report information as I become aware of it regarding clients, the potential for new business add-ons, and client referrals.	
Understanding Impact & Business Issues	I will ensure that all employees understand their impact on the BDEB effort and the overall bottom line.		I will become an expert and valued resource on topics relevant to business.	I will know and comfortably use my own information bite that will convey valuable "need to know" company information. I will make it part of my job to understand and be conversant in core services and sample projects.

Continued - individual BDEB roles

Activity	GM/VP	Sales	Project Manager	Staff
Sharing What You Can		I will encourage 100% employee BDEB involvement for my territory.	I will routinely write white papers on my topic(s) of expertise that can be shared with clients, employees, and the media. I will seek opportunities to present various topics at industry conferences and association meetings.	I will treat co-workers like clients. I will read industry or business journals.
Valuing BDEB	[Plus everything listed in "staff" category.]	[Plus everything listed in "staff" category.]	[Plus everything listed in "staff" category.]	I will routinely evaluate how I'm doing using the BDEB Self-Assessment and develop a personal improvement and goal plan.

Activity	How will I be measured?			
	GM/VP	Sales	Project Manager	Staff
Account Profiles	By my ability to ensure the complete collection and routine update of account profiles.	By my ability to include project managers and staff in the development of account profiles & proposals.	By the number of my ongoing contributions to the account profile database. By the amount of information I bring as a result of active note taking during project meetings and "discovery visits".	By my specific contributions to the development and maintenance of account profiles.
Channels of Opportunity™		By my implementation of and follow-up for specific activities planned as a result of my Channels of Opportunity™.		By the number of potential business leads I bring to the table as a result of positively and proactively representing the company to suppliers, clients, prospects, and the community.
Sharing What You Can			By the number of white papers I write and share with clients, employees, and the media. By the number of opportunities to present to the public that I seek. By the level of client satisfaction during and after each project.	By my knowledge of our information bite. By my ability to effectively deliver our information bite. By the number of opportunities I seek to help employees and clients on special projects (especially those in which my knowledge and expertise can best be utilized.)
Valuing BDEB	By how often I provide performance improvement feedback. By how profitable we are in my geographic area. By the amount of new business we bring in.	By the number of business development calls I make. By the number of "discovery" visits I make. By the amount of new business I bring in.		

	What are my necessary BDEB attitudes, skills, and knowledge?			
Activity	GM/VP	Sales	Project Manager	Staff
Account Profiles	Be a mentor for: BDEB principles core services account profiling Performance coaching		Be proficient at gathering information critical to BDEB success.	
Channels of Opportunity™			Be aware of how I can help develop add-on business with existing clients.	
100% Positive and Proactive Representation	Be competent at consultative selling. Be aware of ways I can support 100% employee BDEB involvement. [Plus everything listed in "staff" category.]	Be a mentor to others on overall BDEB principles. Be competent at consultative selling. Be aware of the way I can support Project Managers and Staff on BDEB. [Plus everything listed in "staff" category.]	 [Plus everything listed in "staff" category.]	Be competent on my role-specific BDEB activities. Be aware of RGS core services, market niches, and vision. Be aware of my overall (negative) beliefs about sales and how I can contribute to business development. Be aware of the number of times I have the opportunity to share our company story with my connections.

	What training and development may be necessary for my role-specific BDEB achievement?			
Activity	GM/VP	Sales	Project Manager	Staff
BDEB Achievement	Management Leadership Coaching Mentoring Consultative Selling	Consultative Selling including: Time & Territory Management Presentation Skills Critical Information Gathering Networking	Account Profiling Critical Information Gathering Consultative Selling Business Etiquette Networking	BDEB Awareness Account Profiling Business Etiquette Customer Service

233

Sample Opportunity Focused
Account Profile

Organizational Information		Contact Information		
Department/Agency Name:		Contact #1:		
Address:		Title #1:		
		Direct Line #1:		
		E-Mail #1:		
		Contact #2:		
Phone:	Fax:	Title #2:		
Web Site:		Direct Line #2:		
# of Years in Operation:		E-Mail #2:		
# of Employees:		Contact #3:		
Type of Operation:		Title #3:		
		Direct Line #3:		
		E-Mail #3:		
Who are their primary customers?		(Make copies of this form for additional contact information.)		
		Regional Information		
		How many field office or divisions in this organization?		
		Please list:		
How are their services delivered to customers?				

Sample Opportunity Focused
Account Profile

Market Factors	Business Issues
Regulatory Issues:	❑ They have some type of business problem. Please specify:
	❑ Their current technical system is no longer meeting client needs. If so, why?
Federal Funding Projections:	❑ They have low customer satisfaction ratings. Please specify:
Competitors:	❑ They do not have enough professional staff for immediate or future work.
	❑ They are on a hiring freeze. If so, why?
Influencing Trends:	❑ Other:

	Organizational Goals or Imperatives
Miscellaneous Information:	Goals:
	Vision:

Recommended Reading

The World's Best Known Marketing Secret, Ivan Misner, Ph.D.

Word-of-Mouth Marketing, Jerry Wilson

Permission Marketing, Seth Godin

Transforming the Way We Work, Edward M. Marshall

The Greatest Sales Stories Ever Told, Robert Shook

301 Great Management Ideas, Bob Nelson

Selling the Invisible, Harry Beckwith

Power Point, Michael Gerber

Talent Solution, Edward Gubman

Measuring Corporate Performance, Harvard Business Review

Every Business is a Growth Business, Ram Charan & Noel Tichy

Open-Book Management, John Case

About the Authors

The references to the word "we" throughout this book are the authors, Linda Sparks and Kris Butler. As partners in Performance Development Company, a business and employee performance consulting firm specializing in improving an organization's business development efforts, they are people who have lived the BDEB principles. They wrote this book to share their ideas regarding *Business Development Is Everyone's Business* because of their shared passion for elevating performance and leveraging all resources within an organization.

Linda Sparks has been a sales representative all of her life. Having owned a business, she relates well with the challenges of business ownership—owning too many hats and not having enough time to wear them! Her proven approaches are documented in this book and can be used with success by both owners and employees. Linda's natural ability as a performance consultant also gives her the edge when it comes to helping others leverage their employees and work environment for successful results.

Kris Butler has had the fortune (or misfortune at the time!) to have worked for various companies who weren't doing "it" well—i.e. marketing, communicating, managing, etc. As a marketing and communications specialist, Kris uses her practical experience and insightful observations to share stories illustrating the principles in this book.

Index

A

B

C

D

E

F

G

H

I

K

L

Langsenkamp Manufacturing, 11—13, 44, 53, 57, 112, 115
Lawrence Sunrise Kiwanis, 159

M

Management support, 197
Managing Transitions (Bridges), 188, 199
Massie, Robert, 89
McDaniel, Michael, 196
McEachern, James, 40
Measurement, 170—177, 179, 183, 213—214
Meetings, 11—12, 66, 90-91, 102, 162, 184
Miramax, 73
Mission statements, 111
Montgomery, Robert, 67
Motivation, 148—149, 190, 192
Mullin, Jane, 65

N

National Speakers Association, 101
Negotiation skills, 116—117
Nelson, Denise, 65
Networking, 70, 98

O

Odetics Corporation, 153
Opportunity-focused contact, 39

P

Passion, 120—121
Performance, 133—135, 160
    Performance benchmarks, 174
    Three levels of proficiency, 211-212
Peters, Tom, 122
    Liberation Management, 22
    Reinventing Work: Professional Service Firm 50, 136

R

S

T

Teachable points of view, 152
Technical Assistance Research Program, 73
The Talent Solution (Gubman), 170
The Tipping Point (Gladwell), 158
301 Great Management Ideas, (Brokaw), 116
Trade shows, 11, 91, 94
Transforming Company Culture (Drennan), 16—17
Trust, 33, 164—165
Twain, Mark, 195

U

Understanding impact, 111, 146—147, 214
        Principle Four, 105, 189
USA Group, 109, 119

V

Valuing BDEB, 156—158, 160—164, 169, 179, 183
        Principle Six, 155, 189
Vendors (see Suppliers)
Volunteering, 49

W

Walker Information, 202
1001 Ways to Reward Employees (Nelson), 176
Wooden, John, 207
Word-of-Mouth Marketing (Wilson), 38, 92—93
Work environment development, 125, 146, 205—206

Z

Zingerman's Delicatessen, 116

Are you practicing
Business Development is
Everyone's Business?

If you're seeing positive results from BDEB
activities in your organization—or, if you know
of a company who is practicing BDEB with
outstanding results—we want to hear from you!

Send us your story about how sales, customer service,
profits, employee retention, etc., has been positively influenced by BDEB, and your story could be featured in our
next book. We'd like to know the following details:

• Who or what positively influenced the situation?
• In what situation was the activity performed?
• What was the result?
• Your name, company name, address, phone number, and
e-mail address
• Your preferred method of contact (i.e., phone or e-mail)

Mail your story to Performance Development Company at
9801 Fall Creek Rd., PMB 347, Indianapolis, IN 46256.
Or, e-mail us at pdc@performancedevelopment.net. Once
we receive your story, we'll contact you to gather more
details. All stories will have facts checked and will only be
published with appropriate authorization. If you have any
questions, call us at (317) 335-2100. Thank you!

Business Development is Everyone's Business

Order Form

Telephone orders: Call (317) 335-2100. We'll want to know how many books you'd like to order and where they should be shipped.

E-mail orders: pdc@performancedevelopment.net

Fax orders: (317) 335-3291. Complete and fax this form.

Mail orders: Performance Development Company, 9801 Fall Creek Rd., PMB 347, Indianapolis, IN 46256. USA. Telephone: (317) 335-2100.

☐   I wish to purchase _____ copies of the book, *Business Development is Everyone's Business* at $19.95 per copy.

☐   I am interested in booking a speaker on the topic of B*usiness Development is Everyone's Business.*

Shipping: U.S: Please add $4 for first book and $2 for each additional book.
International: Please add $9 for first book and $5 for each additional book.
Sales Tax: IN residents only, add 5% state sales tax to total order.
Make Check Payable To: Performance Development Company and send with completed order form to 9801 Fall Creek Rd., PMB 347, Indianapolis, IN 46256.

(Please print clearly.)

SHIP TO

Name _____ Title _____

Company _____

Address _____

City _____ State _____ Zip _____

Phone _____ Fax _____

E-Mail _____

BILLING ADDRESS

Only complete below if your credit card BILLING ADDRESS is different than SHIP TO address above.

Name _____

Company _____

Address _____

City _____ State _____ Zip _____ Phone _____

CREDIT

Credit Card   ☐ Visa   ☐ Mastercard   Exp. Date _____

Credit Card Number _____

Signature _____

Total Amount Enclosed _____